Atlas of Experimentally-Induced Neoplasia in the Beagle Dog

Contributing Authors

Stephen A. Benjamin, D.V.M., Ph.D.
Colorado State University

Gerald E. Dagle, D.V.M., Ph.D.
Pacific Northwest National Laboratory
Currently at Washington State University—Tri Cities

Thomas E. Fritz, D.V.M.
Argonne National Laboratory

Nancy A. Gillett, D.V.M, Ph.D.
Inhalation Toxicology Research Institute
Currently at Sierra Biomedical Inc.

Patrick J. Haley, D.V. M., Ph.D.
Inhalation Toxicology Research Institute
Currently at Nycomed Inc.

Fletcher F. Hahn, D.V.M., Ph.D.
Inhalation Toxicology Research Institute

Bruce A. Muggenburg, D.V.M., Ph.D.
Inhalation Toxicology Research Institute

Roy R. Pool, D.V.M., Ph.D.
University of California, Davis

Thomas M. Seed, Ph.D.
Argonne National Laboratory
Currently at Armed Forces Radiobiology Research Institute

Glenn N. Taylor, D.V.M., Ph.D.
University of Utah

David V. Tolle, M.S.
Argonne National Laboratory

Edited by
Gerald E. Dagle, D.V.M., Ph.D.
Charles R. Watson, Ph.D.
Pacific Northwest National Laboratory

BATTELLE PRESS

Columbus • Richland

PACIFIC NORTHWEST NATIONAL LABORATORY
operated by
BATTELLE
for the
UNITED STATES DEPARTMENT OF ENERGY
under Contract DE-AC06-76RLO 1830

Library of congress Cataloging-in-Publication Data

Atlas of experimentally-induced neoplasia in the beagle dog /
    by the U. S. DOE Task Group on Biological Effects ; edited by Charles R. Watson, Gerald E. Dagle.
        p. cm.
    Includes bibliographical references and index.
    ISBN 1-57477-025-X (perfect bound : alk. paper)
    1. Radiation carcinogenesis--Atlases.   2. Beagles (Dogs)--Histopathology--Atlases.   I.
    Watson, Charles R., 1939-   . II. Dagle, Gerald E., 1939-   . III. U.S. DOE Task Group on
    Biological Effects.
    RC268.55.A86 1997
    616.99'4027--dc21   96-46999
                                                                          CIP

Printed in the United States of America

Battelle Press
505 King Avenue
Columbus, Ohio 43201-2693
614-424-6393: 1-800-451-3543
FAX: 614-424-3819

PREFACE

PURPOSE AND GENESIS OF THE ATLAS

Beagle dogs have been utilized extensively in biomedical research (Andersen 1970, Stannard 1988, Thompson 1989). The U.S. Department of Energy's (DOE) Office of Health and Environmental Research (OHER) has sponsored life-span dose-effect radiation studies in beagles at Argonne National Laboratory (ANL); at the Laboratory for Energy-Related Health Research (LEHR), University of California, Davis; at Lovelace Inhalation Toxicology Research Institute (ITRI); at Pacific Northwest National Laboratory (PNNL); and at the Radiobiology Laboratory, University of Utah. Similar studies were conducted at the Collaborative Radiological Health Laboratory, Colorado State University. Reasons for choosing the beagle over other breeds of dogs included their convenient size, good disposition, and low natural incidence of bone tumors. All the beagles used for these studies have been of purebred stock and were raised in the individual laboratories.

Because results from studies in the various laboratories were to be compared, all the investigators strove to use similar nomenclature and criteria to describe biological effects. For this reason, pathologists from these laboratories met on five occasions between 1976 and 1977 to discuss nomenclature and histologic criteria for diagnoses. At these meetings, criteria were discussed for histopathologic description of lesions in bone, liver, lung, hematopoietic and lymphoid tissues, mammary gland, pituitary, testis, and thyroid. To provide further assurance of cooperation among the DOE laboratories involved, DOE organized several Task Groups in 1985, composed of staff members from the laboratories. The Task Group on Biological Effects was asked to standardize nomenclature and diagnostic criteria for pathology; this beagle pathology atlas is the result of that request. The nomenclature used by pathologists in the various laboratories generally follows that given by the World Health Organization (WHO 1974, 1976); however, modifications are occasionally made to accommodate situations specific to beagles. The purpose of this pathology atlas is to document and explain the diagnostic criteria used in these studies.

The atlas describes target organs of particular interest: lungs for radionuclides delivered by inhalation; bones for bone-seeking radionuclides (delivered by inhalation, injection, or oral administration); and hematopoietic and other soft tissues for external irradiation. It should be noted that, in life-span studies, individual lesions generally cannot be considered radiation-induced; the association between radiation and lesions in radiation-exposed beagles is generally made using statistical methods.

This atlas emphasizes histopathologic observations using the light microscope and routine tissue preparation procedures and stains. The text for each organ system chapter was written by collaborating pathologists and was then reviewed by the other authors.

A large database has accumulated on beagles that were studied in these laboratories. For purposes of computer storage and retrieval, a Systematized Nomenclature of Medicine (SNOMED) diagnostic code (a special adaptation of the Systematized Nomenclature of Veterinary Medicine [SNOVET] codes by Palotay and Rothwell 1984) has been provided for each morphologic diagnosis.

The objective of these efforts is to ensure confidence in the comparisons of research results of dose-effect studies in beagle dogs performed in various laboratories. The results of these studies will continue to be published as peer-reviewed journal articles, and many details of the histopathologic diagnoses will be published in those reports. It is also anticipated that newer methods will become available to better understand morphologic changes influencing diagnoses.

Gerald E. Dagle, January, 1993

ROLE OF THE NATIONAL RADIOBIOLOGY ARCHIVES

Chapters for the atlas were written over a period of several years. Those for leukemia and thyroid were completed in 1989. Four were complete by the end of 1992. As the chapters were received, they were edited and standardized in word-processing files. Proofreading copies of the leukemia, thyroid, bone, and liver chapters were returned to the contributing authors and circulated among the others. It was realized from the start that the atlas would be an expensive publication because of the large number of color and half-tone figures. When the atlas was complete, there were insufficient funds in the lifespan beagle study project at PNNL for publication. Therefore, the manuscript and photomicrographs were transferred to the National Radiobiology Archives (NRA) project at PNNL. [The NRA is now part of the U.S. Transuranium and Uranium Registries (USTUR) at Washington State University—Tri Cities (WSU-TC)].

As the beagle studies were being completed, the DOE instigated an archival project to assure that detailed research records would be available for future analysis. The NRA, operated by PNNL for the DOE, is a repository for information about tens of thousands of individual rodents and other animals which were used in long-term radiobiology studies conducted by the U.S. government over the last 50 years. The mission of the NRA is to gather, organize, and catalog data, original documents, and tissues related to DOE radiobiology life-span studies. The NRA has three tasks:

- operate an interlaboratory computerized information system containing a dose-and-effects database to summarize data on individual animals, an inventory database, and a bibliographic database;

- establish a document archive of original (or "record copy") research materials, such as logbooks, clinical notes, radiographic films, and pathologists' observations;

- operate a specimen archive of histopathology blocks, slides, and tissue samples.

The NRA concentrated initially on studies of beagle dogs exposed to ionizing radiation at five DOE laboratories; results for each of more than 6000 life-span-observation dogs have been transferred and are available. Details of major studies comparing strains of mice were transferred from Oak Ridge National Laboratory and Brookhaven National Laboratory; results for nearly 30,000 mice are available. Additionally, the NRA recently acquired records and specimens from a life-span study of almost 4000 rats that inhaled plutonium at PNNL. Life-span biokinetics data on over 300 nonhuman primates are also available.

At its inception, in 1989, it appeared that the primary task of the NRA was to gather electronic information related to radiobiology studies and combine it into a master database system. The studies, conducted over a long time span in many different laboratories, each used a different approach to data management, ranging from handwritten laboratory notebooks to elaborate computerized database management systems. The DOE wanted to be able to combine results from studies in a unified electronic format accessible from a microcomputer. At that time the NRA task was to design and populate a unified database structure.

As experience was gained with users of the combined database, it became very evident that the NRA is much more than a combined, unified database. The NRA is a living, value-added organization which strives to preserve original material and, at the same time, makes it readily available to new users. The users need access to original data files and documentation to supplement their use of the unified database, and we must carefully distinguish between the original information and the value-added standardization provided by the archival service.

The NRA is selective in scope. The goal is to characterize and preserve the key radiobiological experiments, especially those that are large and costly, which will never be repeated. New studies are added at the concurrence of the advisory committee. When a study is nominated for inclusion, we consider the availability of materials. The optimal approach is to be able to collect electronic data,

written documents, histopathology slides and paraffin blocks, tissues, radiographs, and other materials—in order to provide the entire spectrum of materials for interpretation by new analytical or statistical techniques. In other words, a slide collection is useless without extensive supporting documentation, preferably in the form of a computer database. On the other hand, a database without a slide collection can provide a valuable addition to our collection because it can be combined with other databases in cross-cutting analyses.

The formation phase of the NRA is essentially complete; no significant studies are expected to be added. A detailed description of NRA holdings, and those of parallel archival efforts in Europe and Japan is available (Gerber et al. 1996). The project is phasing into a maintenance/user service mode and its collections and service activities are being merged with those of the USTUR under the direction of Dr. Ronald L. Kathren at WSU.

The NRA was the logical custodian of the atlas because it maintains the centralized copy of the beagle data. Furthermore, as described in the Appendix, the NRA had been involved over the years with most of the authors in efforts to develop the SNODOG beagle-specific variant of SNOVET. It was planned to supply Archives users with photocopies of the atlas text and selected photomicrographs on an individual basis in conjunction with future retrievals of subsets of the database. However, in the summer of 1996, it became apparent that cost savings from other NRA activities were available and we determined to produce the atlas in full as envisioned by its authors.

EDITORIAL CONSIDERATIONS

Prepublication editing in 1996 included further standardization of format, consistent numbering of figures, addition of a list of acronyms and an index. A table was added to each chapter to present the nomenclature, a list of figures, and corresponding SNODOG codes (used in the NRA database) in a convenient format.

There are five chapters dealing with bone, myeloid leukemia, liver, lung, and thyroid. Each chapter is self-contained and consists of narrative descriptions and references, followed by a group of figures. Although it might have been more convenient for the reader if figures were interposed within the text, it was more economical to place them together at the end of each chapter.

The original intent was to provide the atlas in loose-leaf format with 3-ring binders to facilitate periodic supplements. For a number of reasons, it is highly unlikely that any formal, supplements will be forthcoming; therefore, the present binding was selected. It is the authors' intent to continue to collaborate and advise each other of changes and additions. Readers are urged to consult with chapter authors about possible postpublication changes in nomenclature or diagnostic technique. To facilitate such communication, the Author Index contains current addresses.

The delay between chapter preparation and publication complicated the review process for the completed atlas. Since there was insufficient time for review by the contributing authors, and since many of the contributing authors have relocated, final proofreading was performed by Chuck Watson and Dvara-Lee Felton in August, 1996.

Charles R. Watson, August, 1996

REFERENCES

Andersen, A. C., ed. 1970. *The Beagle as an Experimental Dog.* Iowa State University Press, Ames, IA.

Gerber, G.B, Okada, S., Sugahara, T. and Watson, C.R. 1996. International Radiobiology Archives of Long-Term Animal Studies I. Descriptions of Participating Institutions and Studies DOE/RL 96-72 Office of Scientific and Technical Information, Springfield, VA.

Palotay, J. L., and Rothwell, D. J., ed. 1984. *SNOVET Systematized Nomenclature of Medicine Microglossary for Veterinary Medicine.* American Veterinary Medical Association, Schaumburg, IL.

Stannard, J. N. 1988. Radioactivity and Health, A History (DE88013791) Office of Scientific and Technical Information, Springfield, VA.

Thompson, R. C. 1989. *Life-Span Effects of Ionizing Radiation in the Beagle Dog.* Pacific Northwest National Laboratory, Richland, WA.

World Health Organization. 1974. International histological classification of tumours of domestic animals. *Bull. WHO* 50:1-144.

World Health Organization. 1976. International histological classification of tumours of domestic animals. *Bull. WHO* 50:145-282.

ACKNOWLEDGMENTS

The editors are deeply appreciative of the editorial efforts of Raymond W. Baalman, Jr. and Dvara-Lee Felton. They were responsible for organization and preservation of the text and illustrations for many years.

CONTENTS

Atlas
of
Experimentally-Induced
Neoplasis
in the
Beagle Dog

CHAPTER 1: Tumors of Bone

Nancy A. Gillett
Inhalation Toxicology Research Institute
(Currently at Sierra Biomedical Inc.)

Roy R. Pool
University of California, Davis

Bruce A. Muggenburg
Inhalation Toxicology Research Institute

INTRODUCTION

Many of the radionuclides used in the various life-span studies performed in beagle dogs were bone-seekers, for which the predominant late effect observed was primary bone cancer. This chapter discusses the types of bone tumors observed. Because beagles have been shown to have a very low rate of spontaneous bone cancer, the vast majority of these tumors are presumed to be radiation-induced (Pool, Hilliams, and Goldman 1973). The classification scheme used for the bone tumors is that described by Pool in the 3rd edition of *Tumors of Domestic Animals* (Pool, 1990). The majority of the spontaneous tumor phenotypes are represented among the radiation-induced tumors and will be discussed subsequently. Those tumor phenotypes that were not observed in the beagle life-span studies are not presented in this chapter. Radiographs are included where possible; radiographs frequently are invaluable in the clinical diagnosis of bone cancer and illustrate the lytic (destructive), productive, or mixed (destructive and productive) bone lesions produced by the various types of bone tumors. Radiographs also delineate the anatomic location of bone tumors, which can be characteristic of the bone tumor phenotype.

The classification used here is that developed by Pool as a modified version of the one developed by Dahlin and Unni (1977) for categorizing primary bone tumors in humans (Table 1.1). Osteosarcomas, primary malignant bone tumors in which the neoplastic cells produce tumor osteoid and tumor bone (calcified tumor osteoid), display a wide range of histologic and radiographic patterns, depending upon the amount and quality of matrix produced. Although differences in clinical behavior among the various subclasses of osteosarcoma have not been documented in domestic animals, this classification scheme has been useful for distinguishing typical histological patterns in bone neoplasms observed following exposure to bone-seeking radionuclides. Different types of primary bone tumors have developed following exposure of animals to various types of bone-seeking radionuclides given by different routes; these differences are being studied to determine the possible mechanisms of pathogenesis.

Included in this chapter is a brief description of the syndrome of bone lesions termed radiation osteodystrophy. This lesion was frequently observed in bones from radiation-exposed dogs and, in some studies, was consistently associated with sites of tumor production (Pool, Hilliams, and Goldman 1973; Pool, Mortan, and Parks 1983; Nilsson, Morgan, and Book 1985; Hahn et al. 1981). Radiation osteodystrophy has been suggested as a key factor in the induction of the osteosarcomas observed in some of these studies.

Bone

Additional non-neoplastic lesions of bone were not observed routinely; those that did occur were rare spontaneous bone lesions. These lesions have been described in standard veterinary pathology texts and are not discussed in this chapter. Table 1.1 lists the lesions described, corresponding figure numbers, and SNOMED database codes.

Table 1.1. Bone Neoplasia nomenclature, index of figures, and SNODOG database codes.

Nomenclature	Figure(s)	SNODOG Morphology Code[a]
Non-neoplastic		
Radiation Osteodystrophy	1.1–4	M560002
Neoplastic		
Osteosarcoma		M918030
Poorly Differentiated Osteosarcoma	1.5	M918031
Osteoblastic Osteosarcoma		M918730
Nonproductive Osteoblastic Osteosarcoma	1.6-7	M918731
Moderately Productive Osteoblastic Osteosarcoma		M918732
Productive Osteoblastic Osteosarcoma	1.9–10	M918733
Chondroblastic Osteosarcoma	1.11–12	M918130
Fibroblastic Osteosarcoma	1.13	M918230
Telangiectatic Osteosaroma	1.14–15	M918330
Giant Cell Type Osteosarcoma	1.16	M918630
Combined-Type Osteosarcoma	1.17–18	M918530
Chondrosarcoma	1.19–21	M922030
Fibrosarcoma	1.22–24	M881030
Hemangiosarcoma	1.25	M912030
Giant Cell Tumor of Bone	na	M925030
Multilobular Tumor of Bone (Chondroma Rodens)	na	
Liposarcoma	na	M885030
Lymphoid and Myelomatous Tumors		
Lymphosarcoma	na	M961030
Reticulum Cell Sarcoma (Histocytic Lymphoma)	na	M964030
Plasma Cell Myeloma (Multiple Myeloma)	na	M973030
[a] Identical to SNOMED, with addition of shaded 6th digit specific to lifespan beagle studies		

DESCRIPTIONS

Radiation Osteodystrophy

Radiation osteodystrophy is the term used to describe a combination of bone lesions that has been associated with irradiation of bone by internally deposited alpha- or beta-emitting radionuclides. The syndrome is characterized by multiple areas of bone infarction, macroresorption cavities, new bone formation, and marrow fibrosis (Figure 1.1). Bone infarction is identified by empty osteocyte lacunae that may be present within osteons having occluded blood vessels or in osteons having an apparently normal vascular supply. Macroresorptive cavities differ from normal resorption cavities by having larger diameters, more eccentricity of the path of the resorption cavity and orientation to preexisting vascular pathways, and outpockets of osteoclastic resorption extending from the walls of the major resorptive cavity (Figures 1.2; 1.3). The cavities are primarily limited to the diaphyseal cortex. New bone formation occurring in response to alterations in normal cortical structure may be evident in a subperiosteal or inner cortical location (Figure 1.4). Peritrabecular new bone formation is also prominent in some cases. A proliferative, fibro-osseous response is frequently seen in the marrow and often fills some of the resorptive cavities. This response resembles those seen with fibrous dysplasia, ossifying fibroma and osteoblastoma. In severe lesions of radiation osteodystrophy, periosteal involvement may be present and is characterized by periosteal new bone formation and fibrosis. The term radiation osteodystrophy is used to describe this entire spectrum of altered bone remodeling.

The pathogenesis of the lesion appears to be a disruption of the normal remodeling of bone. The resorptive phase of remodeling is "uncoupled" from the bone formation phase. Precursors of osteoclasts, the cells responsible for bone resorption, are located in the bone marrow. Because of the distance between these cells and the site of radioisotope deposition in the bone matrix, the osteoclast precursors are unaffected by the radiation, and bone resorption is essentially normal. In contrast, when the precursor cells responsible for bone formation are irradiated, there is subsequent disruption of normal bone formation. In several studies, radiation osteodystrophy was consistently found at sites of bone tumor formation, suggesting a possible etiologic link between the two lesions. In some studies, radiation osteodystrophy has been regarded as a preneoplastic lesion that evolves into bone tumors (Pool, Hilliams, and Goldman 1973; Pool, Morgan, and Parks 1983; Nilsson, Morgan, and Book 1985). In other studies, radiation osteodystrophy was rarely seen, although bone tumor incidence was high (Gillett et al. 1987).

Osteosarcoma

Poorly Differentiated Osteosarcoma

This tumor is characterized by anaplastic mesenchymal cells that range in appearance from small cells, resembling the reticular cell of bone marrow stroma, to the large pleomorphic cells of undifferentiated sarcoma (Figure 1.5). Small amounts of tumor osteoid are present; small tumor bone spicules may also be present. Because of the paucity of matrix production, these tumors form a very lytic radiographic pattern. Secondary pathologic fractures are not uncommon.

Osteoblastic Osteosarcoma

These tumors are composed of anaplastic osteoblasts and osteogenic precursor cells. The cells are angular, with eccentric hyperchromatic nuclei. The tumors are further subclassified on the basis of the amount of tumor/bone matrix present within the tumor mass. Subclassification is based primarily on histologic examination; however, radiographs are an important ancillary aid that should be used to assess the amount and degree of ossification of tumor/bone matrix present.

3

Bone

Nonproductive Osteoblastic Osteosarcoma

This tumor subtype is characterized by the scant amount of tumor osteoid and tumor bone (Figures 1.6; 1.7). The radiographic pattern is predominantly lytic in bone, with surrounding soft tissue enlargement. In contrast to the poorly differentiated osteosarcoma, which is the primary differential diagnosis for this tumor type, the cells forming the reproductive osteoblastic osteosarcoma are distinctly osteoblasts.

Moderately Productive Osteoblastic Osteosarcoma

An intermediate amount of tumor bone and tumor osteoid is present in this tumor subtype (Figure 1.8) Within an individual tumor, either tumor osteoid or tumor bone may be the predominant matrix. Radiographically, a mixed pattern of destruction and production is characteristic of this subtype.

Productive Osteoblastic Osteosarcoma

Extensive matrix production is evident within tumors of this subtype (Figure 1.9). Abundant, often well-differentiated tumor bone is frequently present. Radiographically, these tumors are very productive and may appear to be sclerotic (Figure 1.10). In the beagle life-span studies, radiation osteodystrophy was often contiguous with tumors of this subtype, and often, no clear distinction between neoplastic and dysplastic bone was apparent.

Chondroblastic Osteosarcoma

The key feature of this osteosarcoma subtype is that the malignant cells directly produce both tumor bone matrix and tumor cartilage matrix (Figure 1.11). This is in contrast to a chondrosarcoma, in which bone spicules may be present, but the bone spicules are formed by endochondral ossification of the neoplastic cartilage matrix. Because of the mixture of matrix patterns present, these tumors have a mixed pattern on radiographic examination (Figure 1.12).

Fibroblastic Osteosarcoma

Tumors of this subtype have regions of a spindle cell population with variable degrees of matrix production, thus resembling a fibrosarcoma (Figure 1.13). In addition, however, neoplastic cells can be identified that are directly producing osteoid or bone matrix. The radiographic appearance of this tumor is dependent upon the relative amount of fibroblastic regions, as well as the amount and degree of mineralization of the neoplastic osteoid. In general, the radiographic appearance is that of a lytic bone lesion.

Telangiectatic Osteosarcoma

Typically this tumor subtype is identified by large, bloody, cystic lesions that are apparent on gross examination, and are identical to the gross lesion produced by a hemangiosarcoma (Figure 1.14). On histologic examination, neoplastic cells, which are usually spindle-shaped, line large, blood-filled cystic spaces within the tumor mass. In addition, tumor osteoid and bone matrix are produced by the same population of neoplastic cells. As one would expect, this tumor has a very osteolytic pattern radiographically. Another histologic pattern for telangiectatic osteosarcomas was identified in beagles exposed by inhalation to $^{90}SrCl_2$ (Gillett et al. 1987). In these tumors, neoplastic spindle-shaped cells formed small capillary spaces in addition to producing tumor bone matrix (Figure 1.15). The vascular component was primarily identified by the presence of the neoplastic cells lining capillary-like structures; however, large, blood-filled cystic spaces were rarely the distinguishing feature of these tumors.

4

Giant Cell Type Osteosarcoma

This tumor subtype is characterized by the presence of numerous tumor giant cells (Figure 1.16). Osteoid and tumor bone matrix are frequently minimal, and, in general, the tumor resembles the nonproductive ostcoblastic osteosarcoma. A lytic bone lesion is present radiographically. This tumor subtype occurred very rarely in the beagle life-span studies.

Combined-Type Osteosarcoma

If more than two of the matrix patterns described above are present, the osteosarcoma is classified as a combined-type osteosarcoma (Figure 1.17). Within the beagle life-span studies, this diagnosis was common and usually resulted from the presence of fibroblastic, osteoblastic, and chondroblastic matrix within the neoplastic mass. The majority of these tumors produce a mixed radiographic pattern (Figure 1.18).

Chondrosarcoma

The distinguishing feature of a chondrosarcoma is the production of varying amounts of chondroid and fibrillar matrix by the neoplastic cells (Figure 1.19). An important criterion is that the sarcomatous cells never directly produce neoplastic osteoid or bone; this is a feature seen only with osteosarcomas (see chondroblastic osteosarcoma, above). If bone is present in a chondrosarcoma, it is formed secondarily as a result of endochondral ossification following resorption of the tumor matrix. Histologically the tumor is characterized by abnormal cartilage cells, with plump, atypical, hyperchromatic nuclei. Mitotic figures may or may not be present. Binucleate or multinucleated cells, or the presence of lacunae containing more than one cartilage cell, are frequently the only morphologic indication of cell division (Figure 1.20). The amount of chondroid matrix produced by different chondrosarcomas is frequently quite variable. When the matrix becomes secondarily fibrillar and hyalinized, morphologically resembling osteoid, or when endochondral ossification occurs, it may be difficult to distinguish the chondrosarcoma from an osteosarcoma.

The radiographic appearance of a chondrosarcoma is frequently variable, and, often, a chondrosarcoma cannot be differentiated from an osteosarcoma (Figure 1.21).

Fibrosarcoma

Fibrosarcoma of bone is a malignant neoplasm of the fibrous connective tissue, originating from stromal elements (Figures 1.22; 1.24). A variable amount of collagenous matrix is produced, but neither neoplastic bone nor cartilage is present. It may be difficult to differentiate this tumor from a fibroblastic osteosarcoma of low osteogenic potential. As would be anticipated, these tumors produce a lytic radiographic lesion, although in some instances only soft-tissue swelling is found. Usually a fibrosarcoma evokes a milder, periosteal response than that observed with an osteosarcoma. Histologically, the tumors resemble fibrosarcomas occurring elsewhere in the body. The majority of these tumors are well-differentiated; occasionally, the tumor may be anaplastic and highly cellular, making it difficult to distinguish it from a poorly differentiated osteosarcoma or nonproductive osteoblastic osteosarcoma. Using special stains, neither cross-striations in the cytoplasms nor evidence of alkaline phosphatase activity can be identified in this neoplasm.

Hemangiosarcoma

The hemangiosarcoma in bone is defined as a malignant neoplasm of endothelial cells, arising from the vasculature of a bone organ (Figure 1.25). This tumor type was not infrequent among some of the beagle life-span studies. Because of the very destructive nature of this tumor, secondary pathologic fractures can occur. Radiographically the tumor appears as a highly destructive lesion, often evoking only a minimal degree of extracortical reactive bone. Histologic characteristics of this

tumor are the same as those observed for a hemangiosarcoma arising in soft tissue. The characteristic feature of this tumor is the formation of vascular channels and spaces lined by neoplastic endothelial cells. The channels may coalesce and enlarge to resemble a cavernous structure. The stroma of a hemangiosarcoma does not form a calcifiable matrix. Telangiectatic osteosarcomas, in which osteoid formation is minimal, may be difficult to distinguish from a primary hemangiosarcoma, particularly if only a small piece of tissue is available for examination.

The remaining bone tumors listed in Table 1.1 (giant cell tumor of bone, multilobular tumor, liposarcoma, and lymphoid and myelomatous tumors) were not identified in beagles exposed to bone-seeking radionuclides. The distinguishing characteristics of these remaining tumors are described by Pool, Hilliams, and Goldman (1973) and Pool (1990).

REFERENCES

Gillett, N. A., B. A. Muggenburg, B. B. Boecker, H. C. Griffith, F. F. Hahn, and R. O. McClellan. 1987. Single inhalation exposure to ^{90}SrCl$_2$ in the Beagle dog: late biological effects. *J. Natl. Cancer Inst.* 79:359-376.

Hahn, F. F., J. A. Mewhinney, B. S. Merickel, R. A. Guilmette, B. B. Boecker, and R. O. McClellan. 1981. Primary bone neoplasms in Beagle dogs exposed by inhalation to aerosols of plutonium-238 dioxide. *J. Natl. Cancer Inst.* 67:917-927.

Nilsson, A., J. P. Morgan, and S. Book. 1985. Investigations of ^{90}SrCl$_2$ in dogs. I. Pathogenesis of radiation-induced bone tumors. *Acta Radiol. Oncol.* 24:95-110.

Pool, R. R., R.J.R. Hilliams, and M. Goldman. 1973. Induction of tumors involving bone in beagles fed toxic levels of strontium 90. *Am. J. Roent. Radium Ther. Nucl. Med.* 118:900-908.

Pool, R. R., J. P. Morgan, and N. J. Parks. 1983. Comparative pathogenesis of radium-induced intracortical bone lesions in humans and beagles. *Health Phys.* 44:155-177.

Pool, R. R. 1990. Tumors of bone and cartilage. In: *Tumors in Domestic Animals* , J. E. Moulton, Ed., 3rd ed. University of California Press, Berkeley, CA. pp. 157-230.

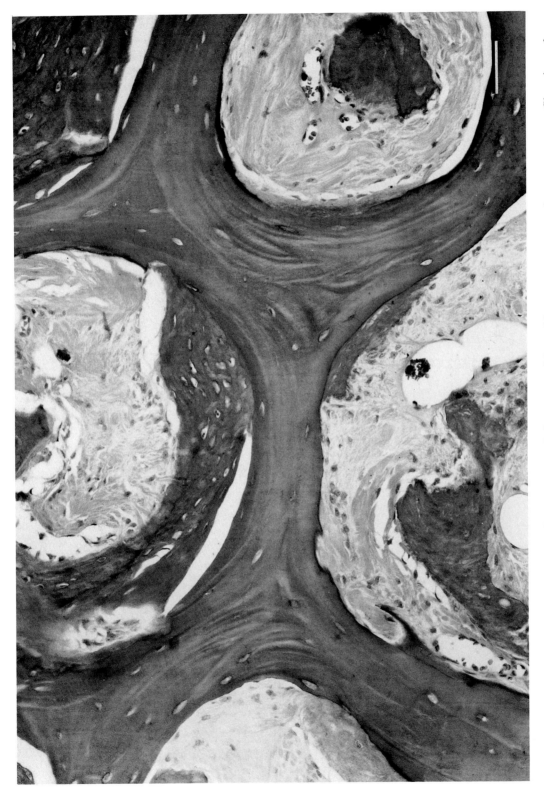

Figure 1.1. Radiation osteodystrophy, note necrotic bone, as evidenced by empty osteocyte lacunae, marrow fibrosis, and peritrabecular new bone formation. *Bar = 50 μm.*

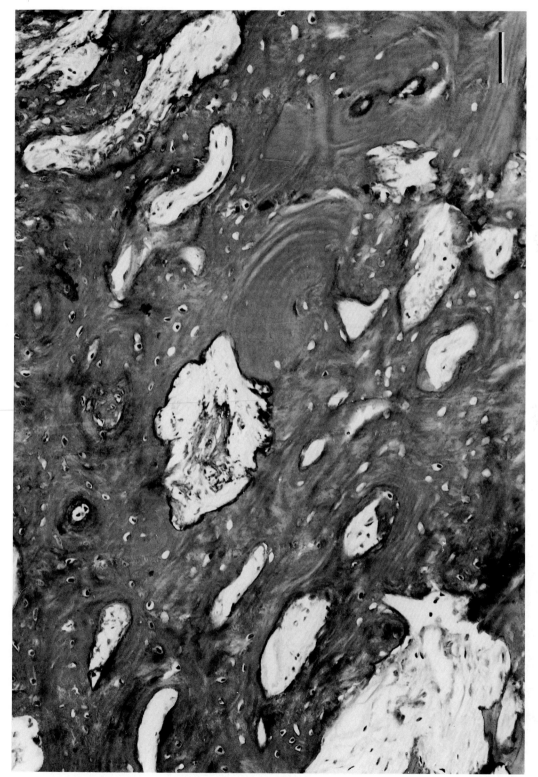

Figure 1.2. **Radiation osteodystrophy:** example of macroresorptive cavities; marrow fibrosis and abundant deposition of woven bone are evident. *Bar = 50 μm.*

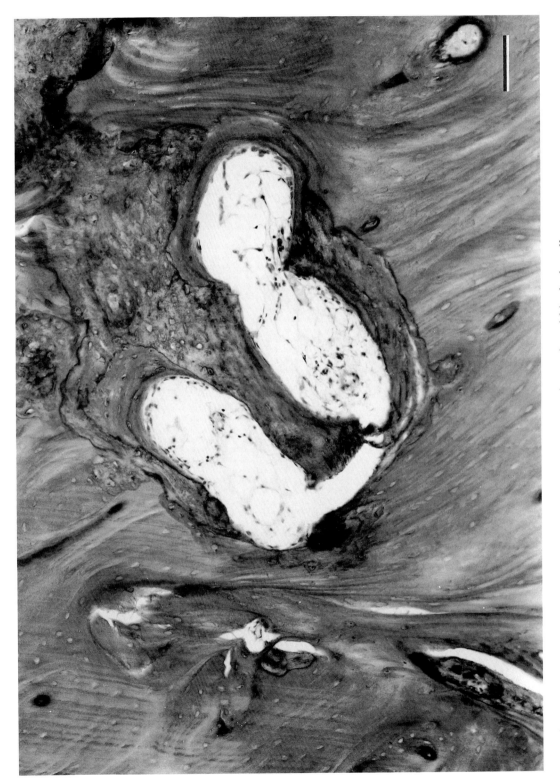

Figure 1.3. Radiation osteodystrophy; note macroresorptive cavity within the lamellar cortex. *Bar = 80 μm.*

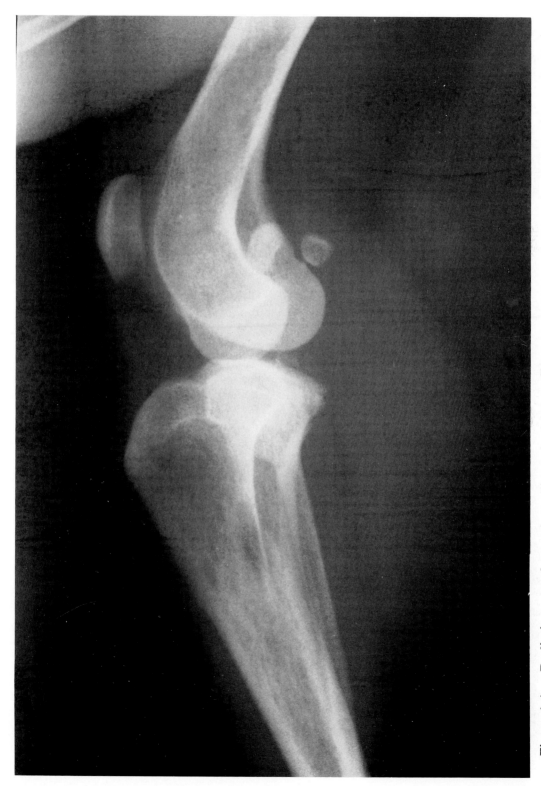

Figure 1.4. **Radiation osteodystrophy**: radiograph of stifle joint. Note multiple areas of punctate osteolysis in proximal tibia.

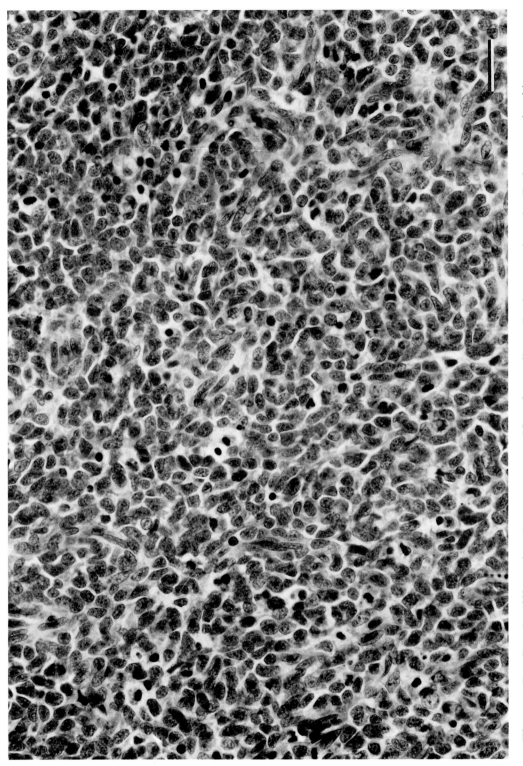

Figure 1.5. **Poorly differentiated osteosarcoma.** Note the small anaplastic mesenchymal cells that comprise this tumor. Rare osteoid formation is present in this tumor, although it is not evident in the photomicrograph. *Bar = 25 μm.*

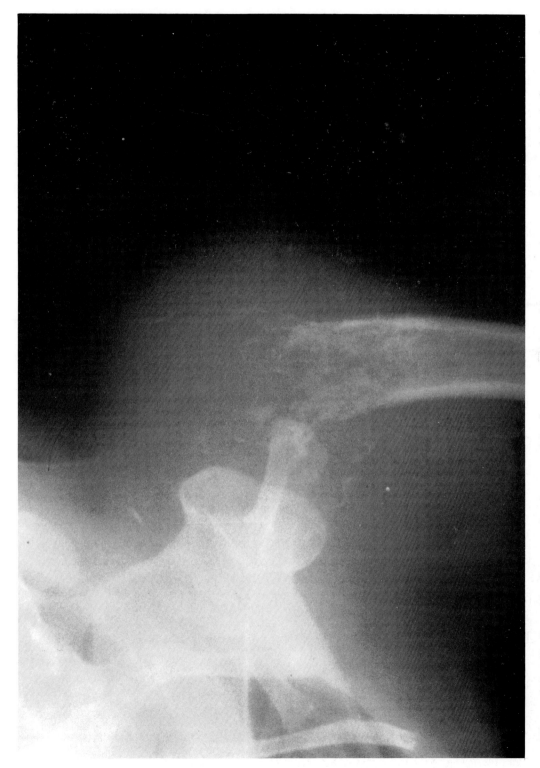

Figure 1.6. Radiograph of **nonproductive osteoblastic osteosarcoma**. Note extensive osteolysis, pathologic fracture and scant evidence of bone production.

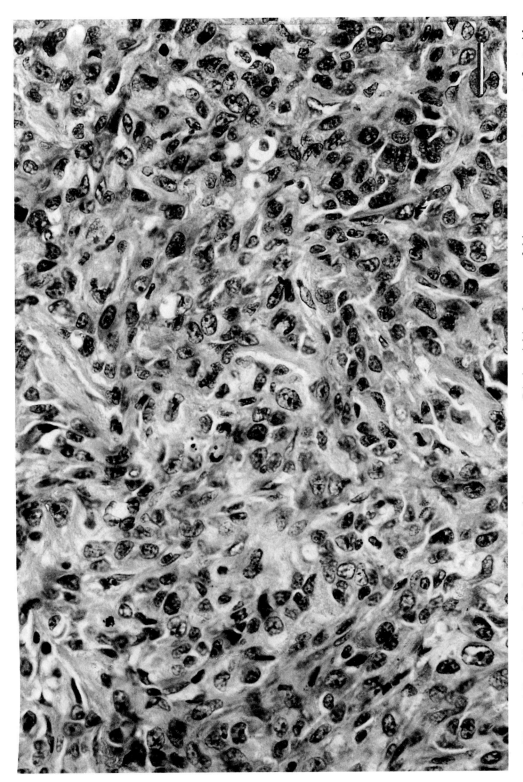

Figure 1.7. Nonproductive osteoblastic osteosarcoma. Distinguishing features of this tumor are: scant amount of osteoid present and cells with cytologic features characteristic of osteoblasts, i.e., angular borders and eccentric nuclei. *Bar = 25 μm.*

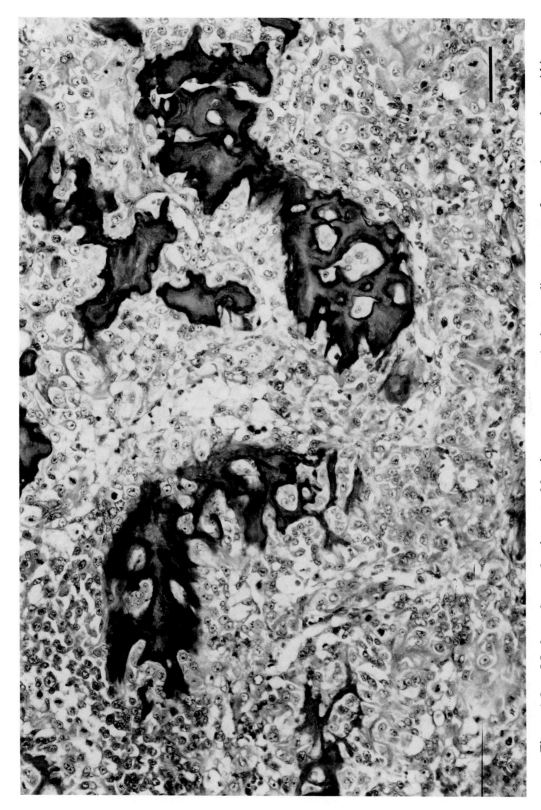

Figure 1.8. **Moderately productive osteoblastic osteosarcoma.** An intermediate amount of tumor bone and osteoid is present. *Bar = 40 μm.*

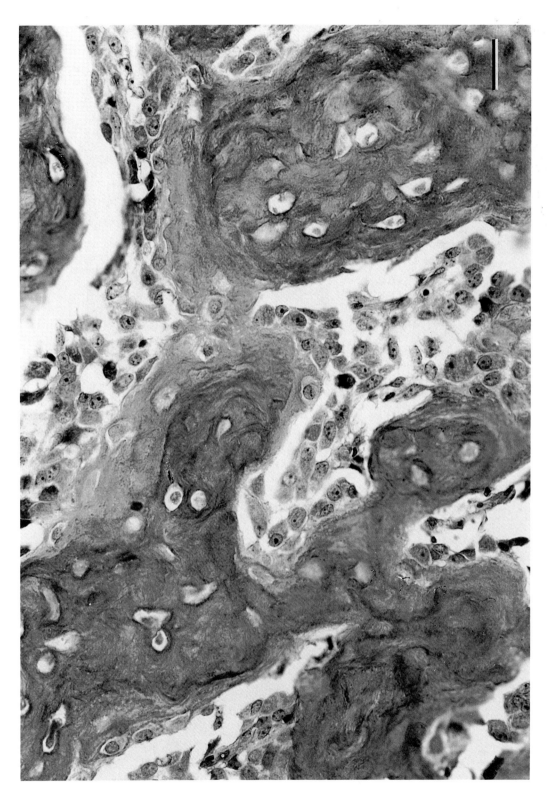

Figure 1.9. Productive osteoblastic osteosarcoma; extensive matrix production with the formation of bony trabeculae. *Bar = 25 μm.*

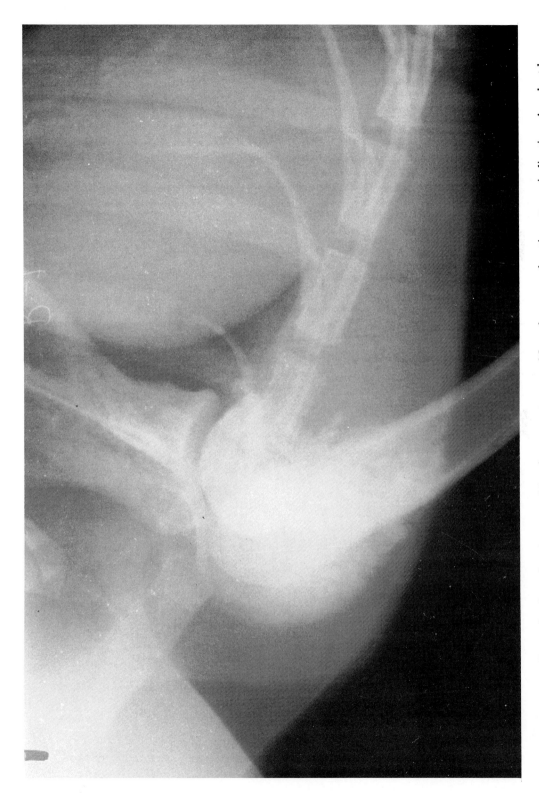

Figure 1.10. Radiograph of **productive osteoblastic osteosarcoma**. Note the very sclerotic pattern, indicating abundant bone formation in the proximal humerus.

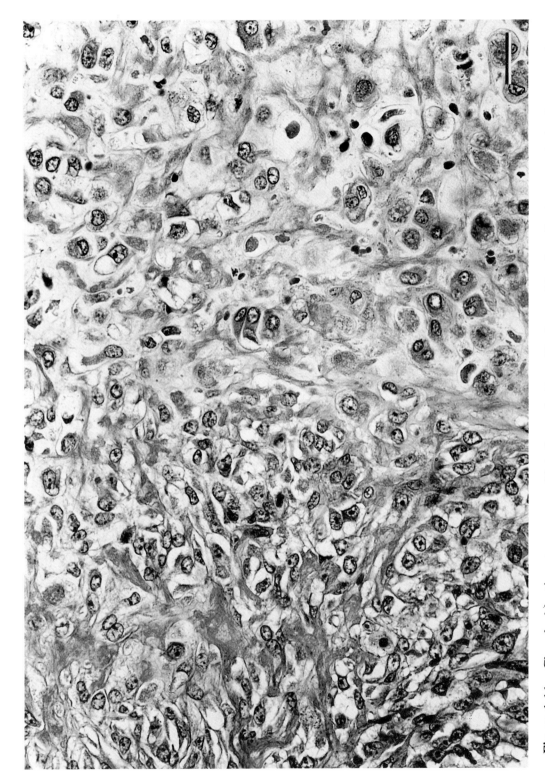

Figure 1.11. **Chondroblastic osteosarcoma**. Note the production of both osteoid and cartilaginous matrix by the neoplastic cells. *Bar = 25 μm.*

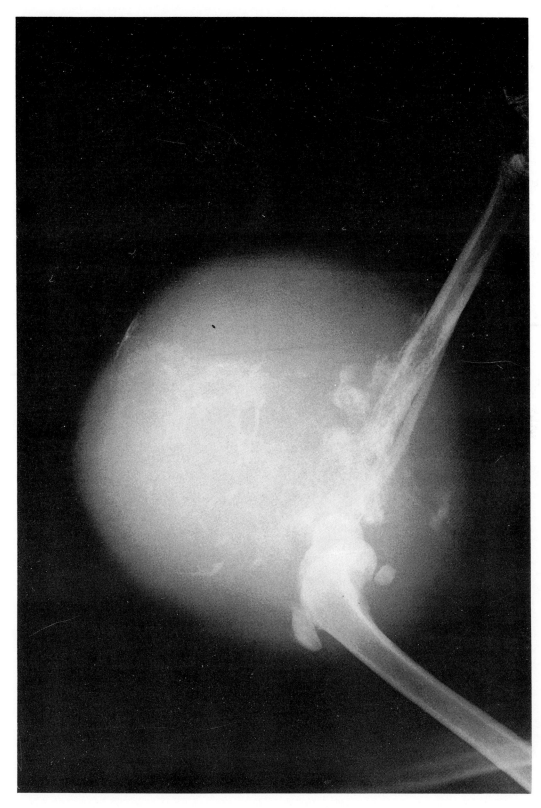

Figure 1.12. Radiograph of **chondroblastic osteosarcoma** in the proximal tibia. Note the predominantly lytic pattern of tumor growth, in addition to evidence of bone production.

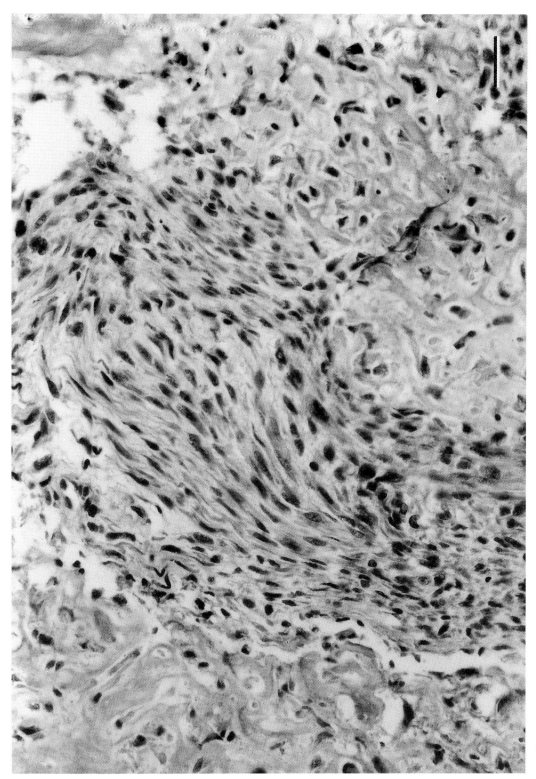

Figure 1.13. **Fibroblastic osteosarcoma.** Note the swirling bundles of spindle-shaped neoplastic cells in addition to the osteoid formation. *Bar = 25 μm.*

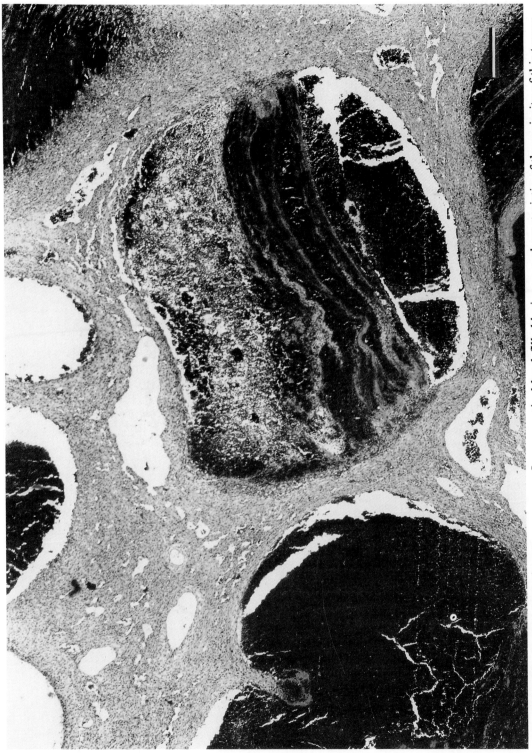

Figure 1.14. Telangiectatic osteosarcoma. Large, cystic, blood-filled lesions are characteristic of the majority of this tumor subtype. *Bar = 150 μm.*

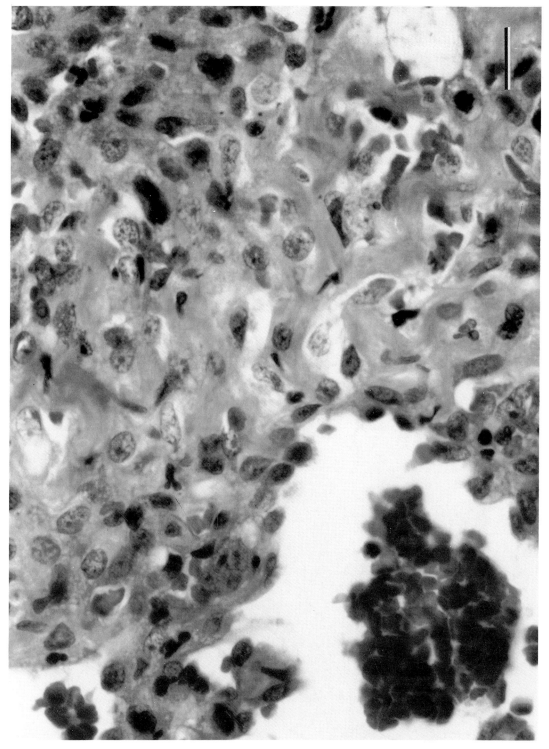

Figure 1.15. Telangiectatic osteosarcoma. Note the osteoid and small vascular channels lined by neoplastic cells. *Bar = 15 μm.*

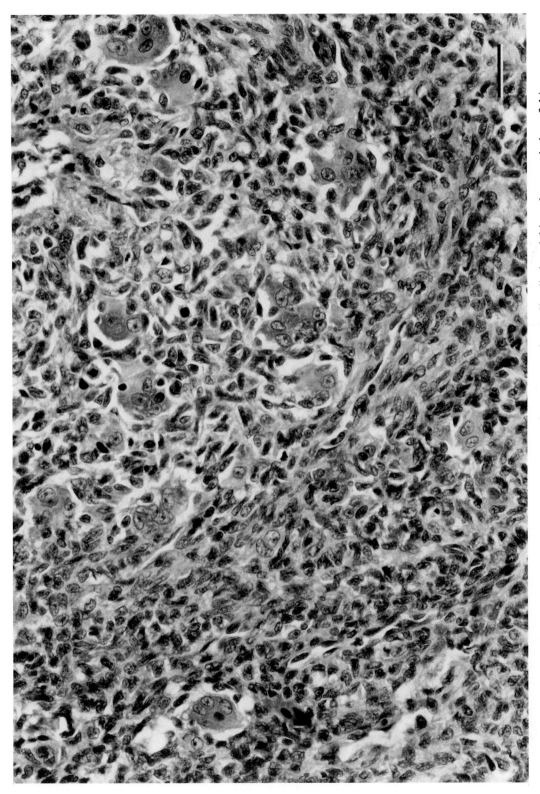

Figure 1.16. **Giant cell osteosarcoma.** Note the presence of numerous giant cells, distinguishing characteristics of this tumor subtype. *Bar = 25 μm.*

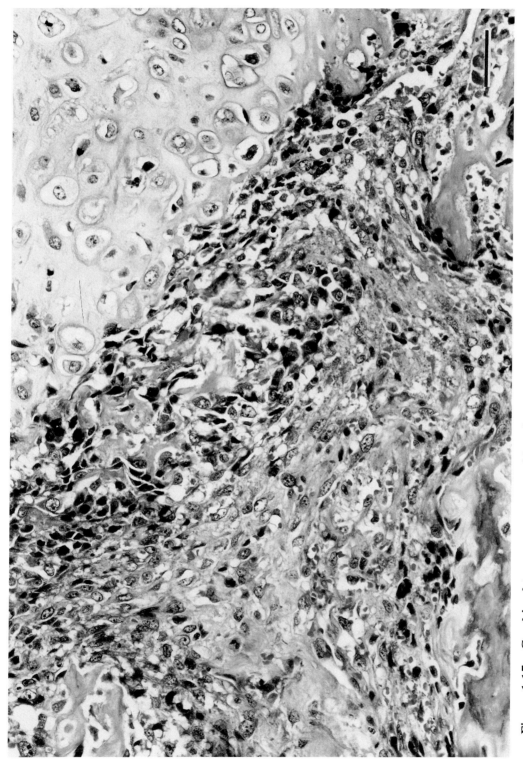

Figure 1.17. Combined-type osteosarcoma. Note the presence of osteoid, cartilaginous, and fibrous matrix. *Bar = 40 μm.*

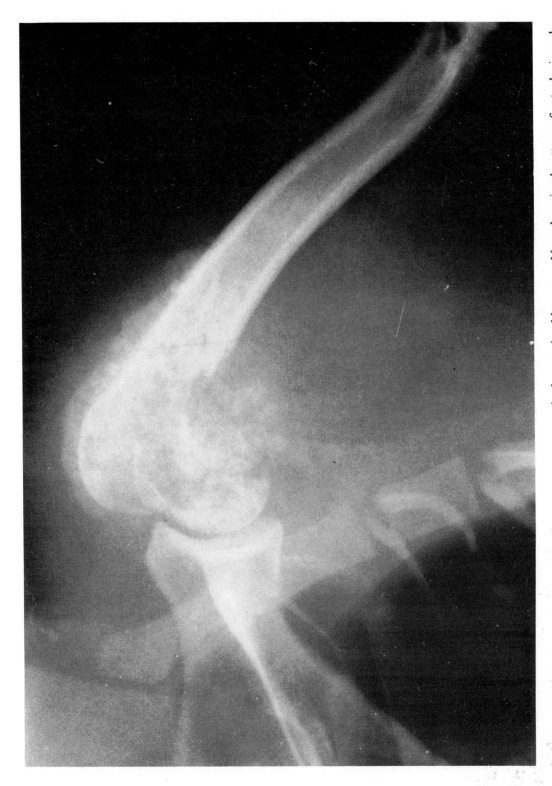

Figure 1.18. Radiograph of **combined-type osteosarcoma** in the proximal humerus. Note the mixed pattern of osteolysis and osteosclerosis.

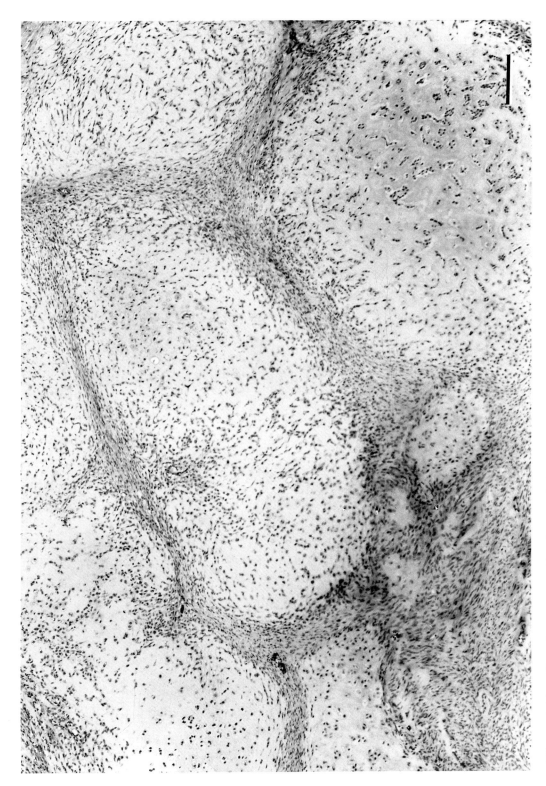

Figure 1.19. **Chondosarcoma**. The characteristic multilobulated pattern of this chondrosarcoma is evident on low magnification. *Bar = 150 μm.*

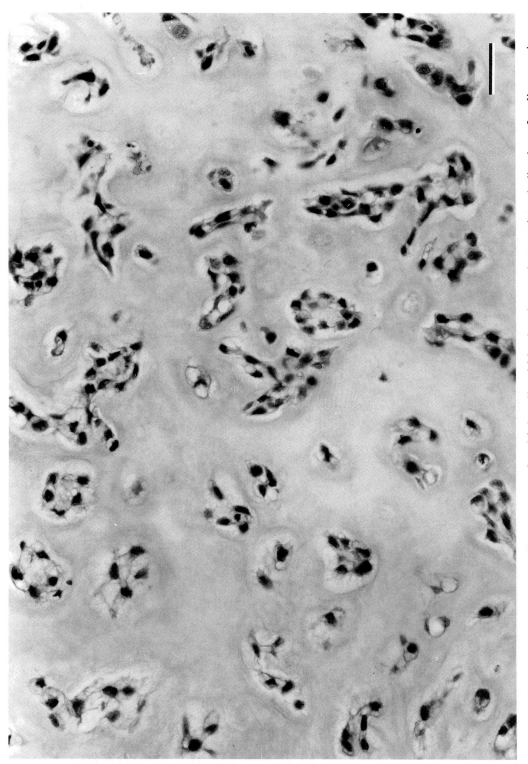

Figure 1.20. **Chondrosarcoma**. The presence of multiple cells within chondrocyte lacunae is an indication of malignancy in this tumor. *Bar = 25 μm.*

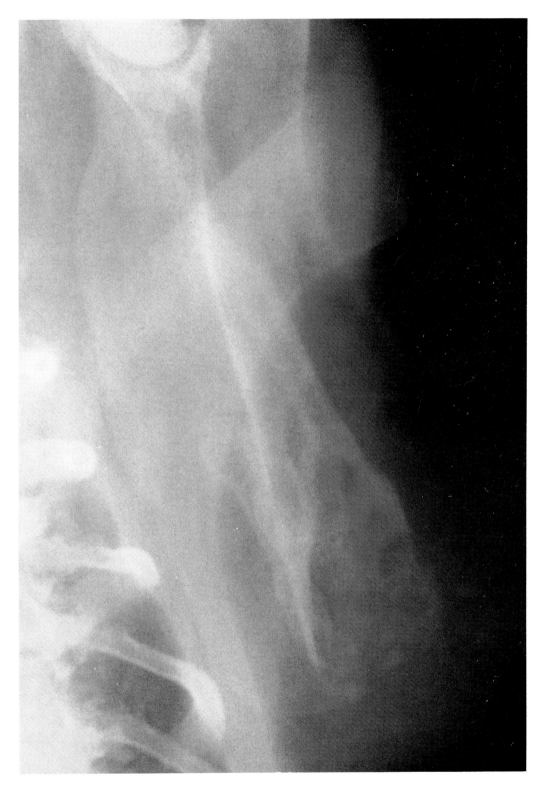

Figure 1.21. Radiograph of **chondrosarcoma** in the scapula. The multilobulated pattern of this tumor produces a characteristic "moth-eaten" lobulated pattern of lysis.

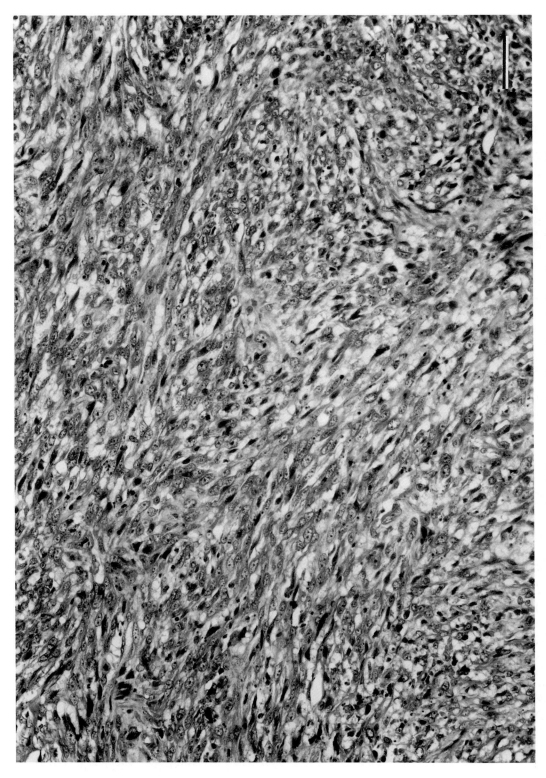

Figure 1.22. Fibrosarcoma. The characteristic interwoven bundles of a spindle cell population are evident. *Bar = 80 μm.*

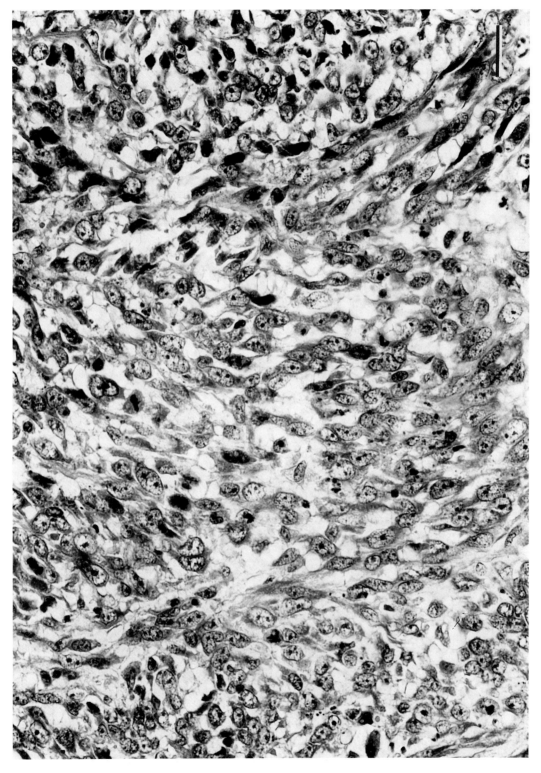

Figure 1.23. Fibrosarcoma. Note that the cells are spindle shaped with a central vesiculate nucleus. *Bar = 25 µm.*

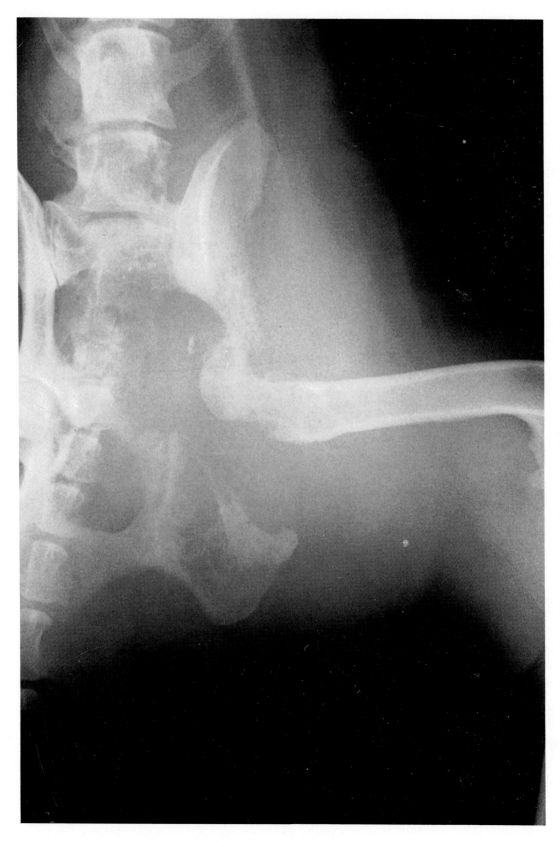

Figure 1.24. Radiograph of a **fibrosarcoma**. Note that only evidence of tumor is osteolysis of the bone and soft-tissue density.

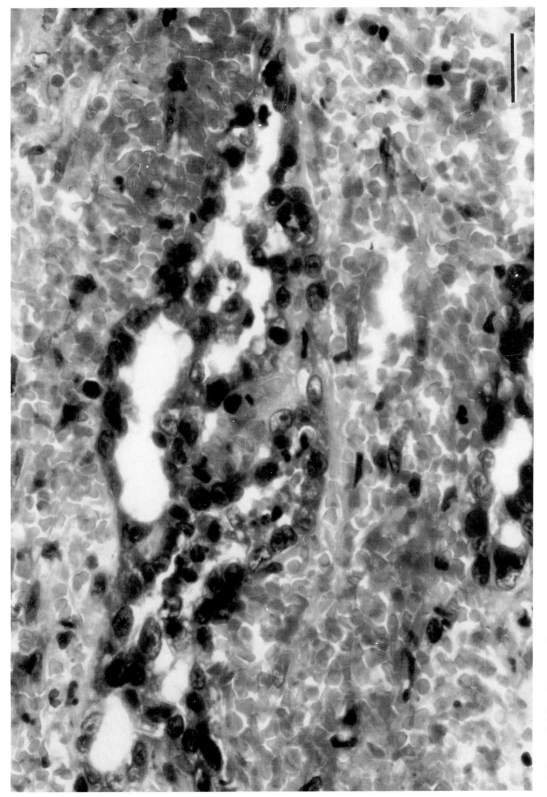

Figure 1.25. **Hemangiosarcoma**. Note the poorly differentiated pleomorphic cells lining small vascular channels. *Bar = 20 μm.*

CHAPTER 2: Radiation-Induced Myeloid Leukemia

David V. Tolle, Thomas E. Fritz, and Thomas M. Seed[1]
Biological and Medical Research Division
Argonne National Laboratory
[1]Currently at Armed Forces Radiobiology Research Institute

INTRODUCTION

The classification used in this atlas chapter is based on the French-American-British (FAB) system for the classification of acute myeloid leukemia in humans (Bennett et al., 1976, 1985a,b). We have made some modifications and additions to include variations observed in the canine leukemia complex that are not addressed by the FAB system. We subdivided FAB-M7 (megakaryocytic leukemia), into M7a (without maturation) and M7b (with maturation); and we added erythremic myelosis (EM). The FAB Codes M1-7 and the corresponding Systemized Nomenclature of Medicine (SNOMED) codes are shown in Table 2.1, along with an index to illustrative figures.

Table 2.1. Myeloid Leukemia nomenclature, index of figures, and SNODOG database codes

Nomenclature	FAB/ANL Classification	Figure(s)	Proposed SNODOG code[a]
Neoplastic			
Myeloid leukemia without maturation	M1	2.1–3	M986131
Myeloid leukemia with maturation	M2	2.4–6	M986132
Hypergranular promyelocytric leukemia	M3	Not seen	
Myelomonocytic leukemia	M4	2.7–9	M986031
Monocytic leukemia without maturation	M5a	2.10-15	M989031
Monocytic leukemia with maturation	M5b	2.16–17	M989032
Erythroleukemia	M6	2.18–22	M984030
Erythremic myelosis	EM	2.23-24	M984031
Megakaryocytic leukemia without maturation	M7a	2.25–26	M991031
Megakaryocytic leukemia with maturation	M7b	2.29–31 2.34–35	M991032
Non-neoplastic			
Myelofibrosis	none	2.32–33	M490005

[a] These suggested codes have not been used in the NRA database; they are SNOMED codes with an additional shaded 6th digit.

Table 2.2 shows dosimetric and clinical details of the 20 illustrative cases. All cases are cytologically and morphologically identified and typed by examination of (a) blood and bone-marrow films and tissue imprints stained with Wright-Giemsa (W-G), and (b) histologic sections of marrow and other tissues. In addition, in many cases, needle aspirates of liver, spleen, and lymph nodes were collected and are available for study. Cytochemistry, as well as both transmission and scanning electron microscopy, was used where needed to confirm diagnosis.

Table 2.2. Selected Exposure History, Terminal Hematology, and Organ Weights for 20 Illustrated Cases

FAB/ANL Classification Incidence [a]	Dog No.	Dose Rate (rad/day) [b]	Days Irradiated	Total Accumulated Dose (rad)	Terminal Hemogram (Days Before Death)			Organ Weights at Necropsy	
					Erythrocytes ×10⁶ /mm³	Leukocytes/mm³ Corrected for Nucleated RBC	Thrombocytes/ mm³	Spleen [c] (g)	Liver [c] (g)
M1 (9.3%)	1212	3.75	1163	4,361	1.83 (0)	10,542	5,000	142.0	406.4
	1381	12.75	1061	13,528	1.23 (0)	44,463	2,000	218.2	477.8
M2 (37.0%)	1472	3.75	1865	6,994	0.89 (0)	39,015	1,000	82.5	344.5
	1678	7.5	405+(250)[d]	3,037	1.37 (1)	12,560	1,000	77.2	416.1
	1913	7.5	405+(576)[d]	3,037	1.15 (3)	64,630	12,000	139.6	891.9
M4 (16.7%)	1394	12.75	1015	12,941	4.49 (1)	41,300	9,000	42.4	407.9
	2405	7.5	200+(1841)[d]	1,500	0.75 (0)	5,381	3,000	310.0	650.0
M5a (5.6%)	1382	7.5	669	5,017	1.81 (1)	7,900	1,000	49.6	275.4
	3241	1.875	1010	1,894	1.50 (1)	39,608	3,000	94.0	458.1
M5b (1.9%)	2331	12.75	117+(1241)[d]	1,492	1.30 (0)	93,627	225,000	49.0	405.0
M6 (14.6%)	1366	3.75	1949	7,309	1.21 (0)	34,148	1,000	188.8	538.0
	1469	3.75	1440	5,400	2.07 (2)	9,677	2,000	221.7	526.8
	2968	1.875	1831	3,433	1.23 (1)	51,264	15,000	200.0	499.8
EM (7.4%)	1439	3.75	1430	5,362	1.73 (1)	18,252	1,000	195.2	449.3
	2976	1.875	1261	2,364	0.87 (0)	8,839	5,000	90.5	548.1
M7a (1.9%)	4124	7.5	688[e]	5,160	2.19 (1)	800	22,000	41.0	236.8
M7b (5.6%)	3255	1.875	841	1,577	1.70 (0)	45,288	90,000	215.0	489.6
	3871	7.5	894	6,705	2.53 (5)	5,300	34,000	40.6	468.0
	3907	7.5	1335	10,012	1.51 (0)	11,584	2,075,000	52.1	447.1
Myelofibrosis [f]	3084	7.5	505	3,787	0.66 (0)	1,400	25,000	26.5	292.0

[a] Incidence of observed cases based on a total of 54 cases of radiation-induced myeloid leukemia. FAB/ANL = French-American - British/Argonne National Laboratory.
[b] Exposures were given 22 hours/day, 7 days/week with a ⁶⁰Co gamma source, commencing at approximately 400 days of age.
[c] The mean weight, ± SD, for 44 adult nonexperimental beagles: Spleen = 24.9 ± 1.2, Liver = 323.2 ± 13.5.
[d] Dogs received terminated exposures; + (days) is number of days surviving following termination of irradiation.
[e] In-utero irradiation from birth minus 63 days.
[f] Total observed nonleukemic cases = 6.
Note: No case of myeloid leukemia has been observed in 292 deceased, adult, nonirradiated, control dogs.

Of the cases discussed here, the terminal hemogram in the majority shows severe anemia and thrombocytopenia. Total leukocyte and differential counts vary from an aleukemic-subleukemic count to a leukemic blast hiatus. Necropsy findings in the majority of cases show moderate to marked hepatosplenomegaly, lymphadenopathy, and pulpy hypercellular marrow. The degree of leukemic cell infiltration in both hematopoietic and nonhematopoietic tissues varies widely. A well-defined preleukemic syndrome is observed in most dogs at periods from 1 month to 2 y prior to death and has been described: Fritz, Tolle, and Seed 1985; Seed et al. 1978; Seed, Chubb, and Tolle 1981; Tolle et al. 1982a,b, 1983. A number of cases in the Argonne study have previously been reported: Fritz, Norris, and Tolle 1973; Fritz et al. 1982; Seed et al. 1977, 1982; Tolle, Fritz, and Norris 1977; Tolle et al. 1979a,b; Tolle, et al. 1979a,b; Tolle et al. 1982a,b.

DESCRIPTIONS

Myeloid Leukemia Without Maturation (FAB-M1) (SNOVET M-98613)

In the bone marrow, the predominant cell is the myeloblast, although there may be a minimal population of later cell stages (promyelocytes and myelocytes). The blast population exceeds 50% of the nonerythroid series, it is nongranular, and it contains one or more prominent nucleoli. A high percentage of blasts may be micromyeloblasts. A small proportion may stain with Sudan black or myeloperoxidase (MPO) (Figures 2.1–2.3).

Myeloid Leukemia With Maturation (FAB-M2) (SNOVET M-98613)

The majority of marrow cells are in the myeloblast-myelocyte stage, although later stages are not uncommon, and in some cases mature neutrophils may be present in large numbers (neutrophilic variant). However, these cells generally show abnormalities, i.e., pseudo-Pelger-Huët segmentation (Fritz, Tolle, and Seed 1985; Tolle et al., 1982b) and hypo- or agranularity (Figures 2.4–2.6).

Hypergranular Promyelocytic Leukemia (FAB-M3)

This condition has not been observed in the Argonne studies and is not described in this atlas.

Myelomonocytic Leukemia (FAB-M4) (SNOVET M-98603)

The marrow shows a predominance of cells of both granulocytic and monocytic differentiation, with the myeloblast-myelocyte stages constituting more than 50% of the nonerythroid series; the monoblast, promonocyte population makes up more than 20%. The peripheral blood shows a high percentage of promonocytes and monocytes, with the monocytes possibly having band-like and segmented nuclei. The combined specific/nonspecific esterase stain is useful in diagnosis (Figures 2.7–2.9).

Monocytic Leukemia Without Maturation (FAB-M5a) (SNOVET M-98913)

The predominant marrow cell is the monoblast, with delicate chromatin, prominent nucleoli, and cytoplasmic buds or pseudopodia. The blast component usually exceeds 80% of the total cell population. A low percentage (10% to 15%) of promonocytes may be present, as well as a minor granulocytic component, which is usually less than 10% (Figures 2.10–2.15).

Monocytic Leukemia With Maturation (FAB-M5b) (SNOVET M-98913)

In the marrow a monoblast-promonocyte hiatus is the prominent feature, but a high percentage of mature monocytes may be found in the peripheral blood. Many of these mature monocytes show band-like and segmented nuclei (Figures 2.16–2.17).

Erythroleukemia (FAB-M6) (SNOVET M-98403)

The bone marrow is characterized by a mixed population of rubriblasts and myeloblasts, with the myeloblast-myelocyte population being less than 25% to 30% of the total nucleated cells. The erythroid series shows severe maturation arrest, asynchronous nuclear/cytoplasmic maturation, megaloblastic features, and giant forms. The later stages, i.e., prorubricytes, rubricytes, and metarubricytes, show bizarre morphologic features such as karyorrhexis, micronuclei, and double nucleated forms. Aberrant mitotic figures may be prominent. A reverse myeloid:erythroid ratio is always seen (Figures 2.18–2.22).

Erythremic Myelosis (EM) (SNOVET M-98403)

The marrow erythroid series shows the same features as in M6, but granulocyte maturation/differentiation is relatively normal, and there is little or no increase in myeloblasts. Micro-megakaryocytes may be present, but cytoplasmic maturation appears to be morphologically normal. The myeloid:erythroid ratio varies widely, but is rarely greater than 1:1 (Figures 2.23–2.24).

Megakaryocytic Leukemia Without Maturation (FAB-M7a) (SNOVET M-99103)

The marrow shows a high percentage (>80%) of megakaryoblasts and micromegakaryocytes. The blast cells vary in size from small round cells with little cytoplasm (which resemble lymphoblasts) to cells that are three to four times larger. The majority have a round nucleus, with fairly dense chromatin and one to four distinct nucleoli. Double-nucleated micromegakaryocytes are not uncommon. Many cells have a somewhat eccentric nucleus. A moderate degree of cytoplasmic vacuolization may be seen and may represent saccules of the developing demarcation membrane system. Mature but aberrant megakaryocytes are present in small numbers, as are mature naked mega-karyocyte nuclei. Acetylcholinesterase (ACHE) stain is helpful in diagnosis on peripheral blood buffy coat and bone-marrow films, and ultrastructural platelet peroxidase is diagnostic in transmission electron microscopic sections (Figures 2.25–2.26).

Megakaryocytic Lukemia With Maturation (FAB-M7b) (SNOVET M-99103)

The predominant marrow cell is the recognizable but highly aberrant megakaryocyte and micro-megakaryocyte. A small percentage of megakaryoblasts is also seen. Large cytoplasmic fragments, giant platelets, and aberrant vacuolated and hypogranular platelets are seen in the peripheral blood. In many cases, there is increased marrow fibrosis, which may result in inadequate material from aspirates for film preparation (Figures 2.27–2.31 and 2.34–2.35).

Myelofibrosis (SNOVET M-49000/T-06000)

Because myelofibrosis is included with the myeloproliferative disorders and is often seen in the myeloid leukemias, particularly the megakaryocytic and chronic myelogenous forms, we have included it in this atlas. Nonleukemic myelofibrosis is a prominent endpoint in our radiation studies, constituting 9.1%, (6/66 cases of either myeloproliferative disease or myelodysplastic syndrome) (Figures 2.32–2.33).

REFERENCES

Bennett, J. M., D. Catovsky, M. T. Daniel, G. Flandrin, D. A. G. Galton, H. R. Gralnick, and C. Sultan. 1976. Proposals for the classification of the acute leukemias. *Br. J. Haematol.* 33:451-458.

Bennett, J. M., D. Catovsky, M. T. Daniel, G. Flandrin, D. A. G. Galton, H. R. Gralnick, and C. Sultan. 1985a. Criteria for the Diagnosis of Acute Leukemia of Megakaryocyte Lineage (M7), A Report of the French-American-British Cooperative Group. *Ann. Int. Med.* 103:460-462.

Bennett, J. M., D. Catovsky, M. T. Daniel, G. Flandrin, D. A. G. Galton, H. R. Gralnick, and C. Sultan. 1985b. Proposed Revised Criteria for the Classification of Acute Myeloid Leukemia, A Report of the French-American-British Cooperative Group. *Ann. Int. Med.* 103:460-462.

Fritz, T. E., W. P. Norris, and D. V. Tolle. 1973. Myelogenous leukemia and related myeloproliferative disorders in beagles continuously exposed to ^{60}Co gamma-radiation. *Bibl. Haematol.* 39:170-188.

Fritz, T. E., D. V. Tolle, D. E. Doyle, T. M. Seed, and S. M. Cullen. 1982. Hematologic Responses of Beagles Exposed Continuously to Low Doses of 60-Co Gamma-Radiation, pp. 229-240. In: *Experimental Hematology Today,* Part VIII. S. J. Baum, G. D. Ledney, and S. Thierfelder, Eds. S. Karger, New York.

Fritz, T. E., D. V. Tolle, and T. M. Seed. 1985. The Preleukemic Syndrome in Radiation-Induced Myelogenous Leukemia and Related Myeloproliferative Disorders, pp. 87-100. In: The Preleukemic Syndrome (Hematopoietic Dysplasia, G. C. Bagby, Jr., Ed. CRC Press, Boca Raton, FL.

Seed, T. M., D. V. Tolle, T. E. Fritz, R. L. Devine, C. M. Poole, and W. P. Norris. 1977. Irradiation-induced erythroleukemia and myelogenous leukemia in the beagle dog: Hematology and ultrastructure. *Blood* 50:1061-1079.

Seed, T. M., D. V. Tolle, T. E. Fritz, S. M. Cullen, L. V. Kaspar, and C. M. Poole. 1978. Hemo-Pathological Consequences of Protracted Gamma Irradiation in the Beagle: Preclinical Phases of Leukemia Induction, Late Biological Effects of Ionizing Radiation, pp. 531-545. Vol. I, IAEA International Symposium, IAEA-SM-224/308, International Atomic Energy Agency, Vienna.

Seed, T. M., G. T. Chubb, and D. V. Tolle. 1981. Sequential Changes in Bone Marrow Architecture during Continuous Low Dose Gamma Irradiation, pp. 16, 61-72. In: *Scanning Electron Microscopy/1981/IV.* O. Johari, R. M. Albrecht, and T. M. Seed, Eds. SEM, Inc., AMF O'Hare, Chicago, IL.

Seed, T. M., G. T. Chubb, D. V. Tolle, T. E. Fritz, C. M. Poole, D. E. Doyle, L. S. Lombard, and L. V. Kaspar. 1982. The Ultrastructure of Radiation-Induced Endosteal Myelofibrosis in the Dog, pp. 377-391. In: *Scanning Electron Microscopy/ 1982/I.* O. Johari, S. A. Bhatt, and I. C. Pontarelli, Eds. SEM, Inc., AMF O'Hare, Chicago, IL.

SNOVET. 1984. Systemized Nomenclature of Medicine, Microglossary for Veterinary Medicine. J. L. Palotay and D. J. Rothwell, Eds. American Veterinary Medical Association, Schaumburg, Il.

Tolle, D., T. E. Fritz, and W. P. Norris. 1977. Radiation-induced erythroleukemia in the beagle dog. A hematologic summary of five cases. *Am. J. Pathol.* 87:499-510.

Tolle, D., T. M. Seed, T. E. Fritz, L. S. Lombard, C. M. Poole, and W. P. Norris. 1979a. Acute monocytic leukemia in an irradiated beagle. *Vet. Pathol.* 16:243-254.

Tolle, D., T. M. Seed, T. E. Fritz, and W. P. Norris, W. P. 1979b. Irradiation-Induced Canine Leukemia: A Proposed New Model. Incidence and Hematopathology, pp. 247-256. In: Experimental Hematology Today, 1979, S. J. Baum and G. D. Ledney, Eds. Springer-Verlag, New York.

Tolle, D. V., T. M. Seed, S. M. Cullen, C. M. Poole, T. E. and Fritz. 1982a. Aberrant Megakaryocytopoiesis Preceding Radiation-Induced Leukemia in the Dog, pp. 367-376. In: Scanning Electron Microscopy/1982/I. 0. Johari, R. M. Albrecht, and T. M. Seed, Eds. SEM, Inc., AMF O'Hare, Chicago, IL.

Tolle, D. V., T. E. Fritz, T. M. Seed, S. M. Cullen, L. S. Lombard, and C. M. Poole. 1982b. Leukemia Induction in Beagles Exposed Continuously to ^{60}Co Gamma-Irradiation, pp. 241-249. In: Hematopathology, Experimental Hematology Today, Part VIII, S. J. Baum, G. D. Ledney, and S. Theirfelder, Eds. S. Karger, New York.

Tolle, D. V., S. M. Cullen, T. M. Seed, and T. E. Fritz. 1983. Circulating micromegakaryocytes preceding leukemia in three dogs exposed to 2.5 R/day gamma radiation. *Vet. Pathol.* 20:111-114.

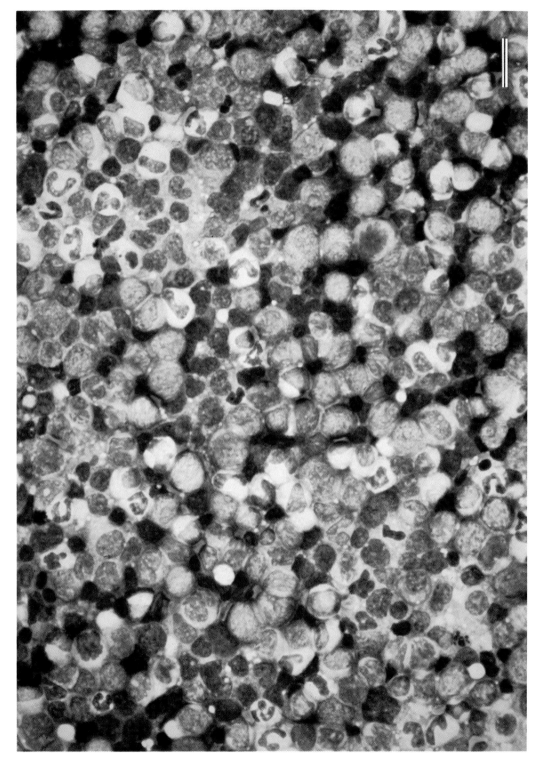

Figure 2.1. **M1 - Myeloid lukemia without maturation.** Terminal bone-marrow imprint showing myeloblast hiatus *(Dog 1381, W-G). Bar = 20 μm. (From Seed et al. 1977, p. 1065. Courtesy of Grune and Stratton, Inc., Orlando, FL).*

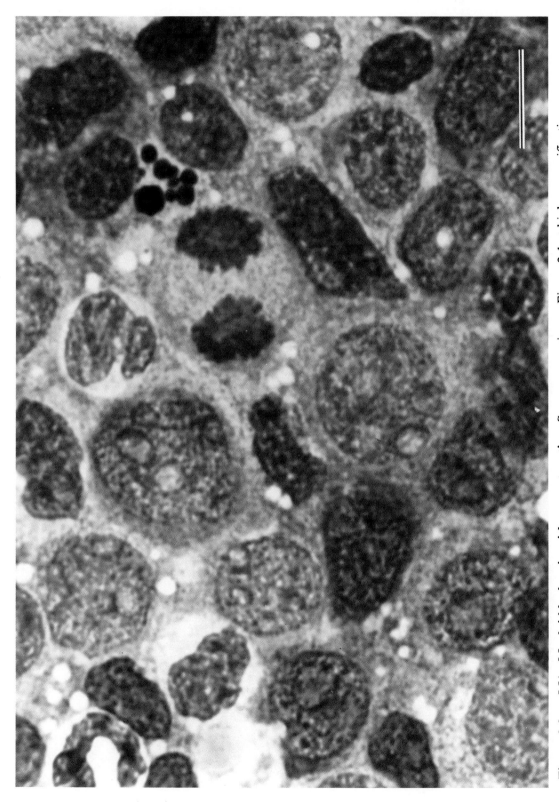

Figure 2.2.   M1 - Myeloid leukemia without maturation. Same preparation as Figure 2.1 at higher magnification. *Bar = 10 μm.*

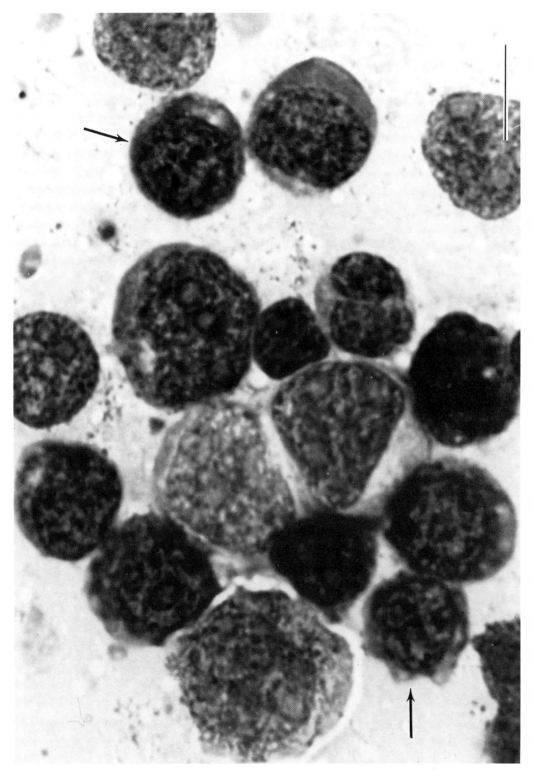

Figure 2.3. **M1 - Myeloid leukemia without maturation.** Terminal bone-marrow imprint showing agranular myeloblasts and micromyeloblasts (→) *(Dog 1212, W-G), Bar = 10 μm.*

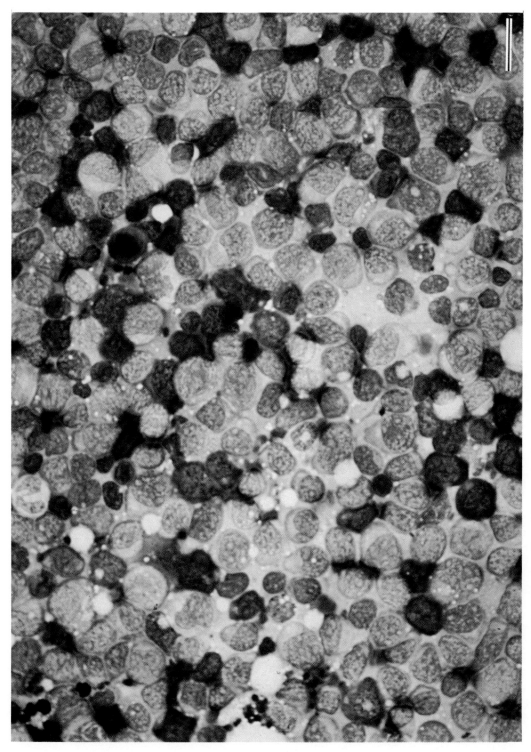

Figure 2.4. M2- Myeloid leukemia with maturation. Terminal bone-marrow aspirate showing some degree of cellular maturation; however, the predominant population consists of cells in the myeloblast to myelocyte stage *(Dog 1472, W-G). Bar = 20 μm.*

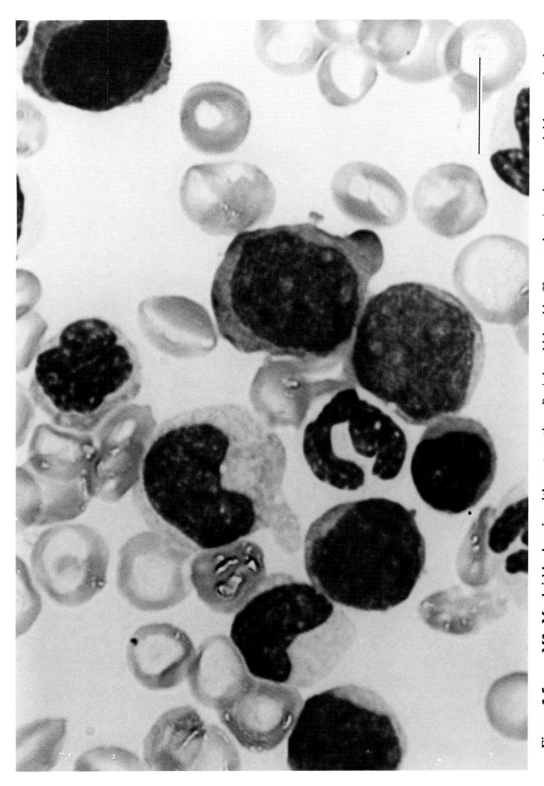

Figure 2.5.   **M2- Myeloid leukemia with maturation.** Peripheral blood buffy coat showing three myeloblasts and other granulocytes in later stages of maturation *(Dog 1913, W-G). Bar = 10 μm.*

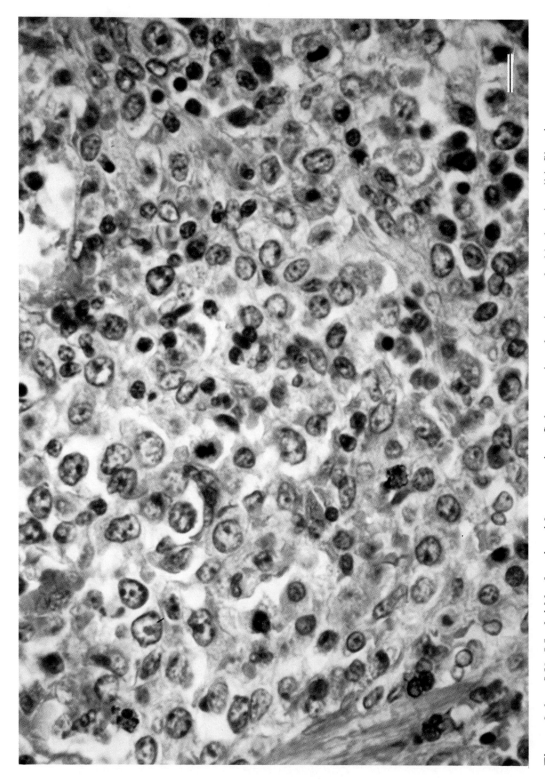

Figure 2.6. **M2- Myeloid leukemia with maturation.** Spleen section showing marked leukemic cell infiltration *(Dog 1678, H&E).* *Bar = 10 μm.*

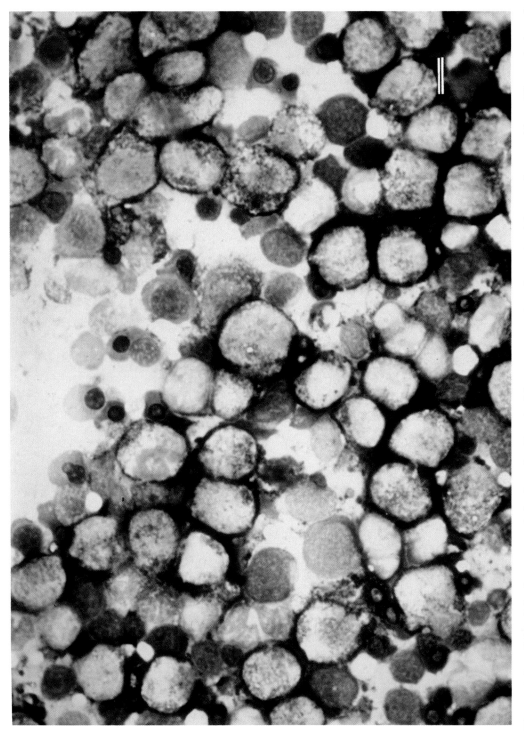

Figure 2.9. **M4 - Myelomonocytic leukemia.** Terminal bone-marrow imprint stained for myeloperoxidase. The majority of cells are myeloperoxidase-positive promyelocytes and myelocytes, with a smaller proportion of monocytic cells. Erythroid elements are still present *(Dog 2405, MPO/W-G). Bar = 10 μm.*

Myeloid Leukemia

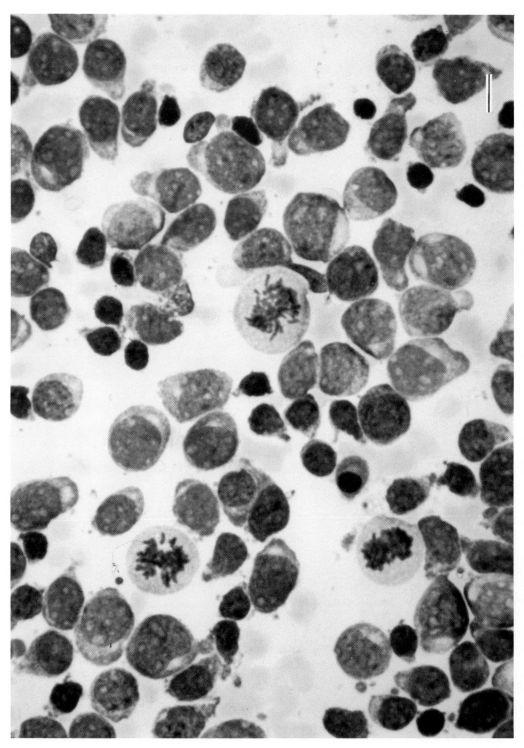

Figure 2.10. **M5a - Monocytic leukemia without maturation.** Bone-marrow aspirate 6 days before death, showing a monoblast hiatus. Note the prominent nucleoli, delicate chromatin, and cytoplasmic buds or pseudopodia *(Dog 3241, W-G). Bar = 10 μm. (From Tolle, et al., 1982b, p. 245. Courtesy S. Karger AG, Basel).*

48

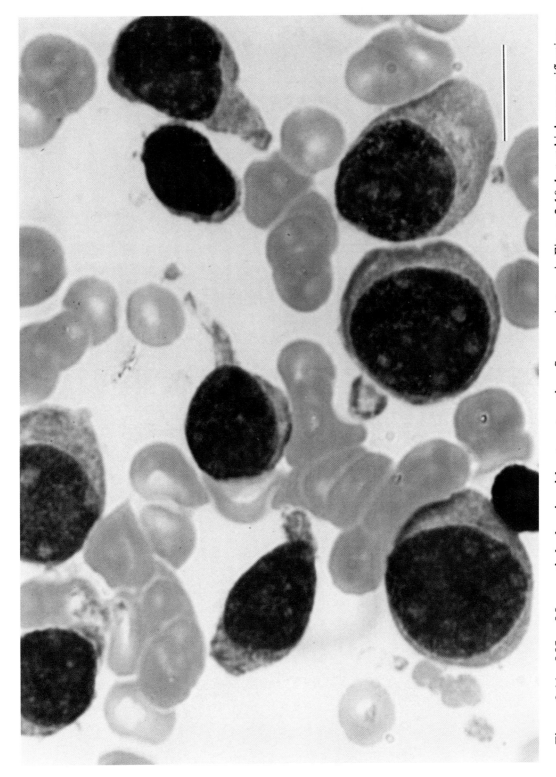

Figure 2.11. M5a - Monocytic leukemia without maturation. Same aspirate as in Figure 2.10, but at higher magnification.
Bar = 10 µm.

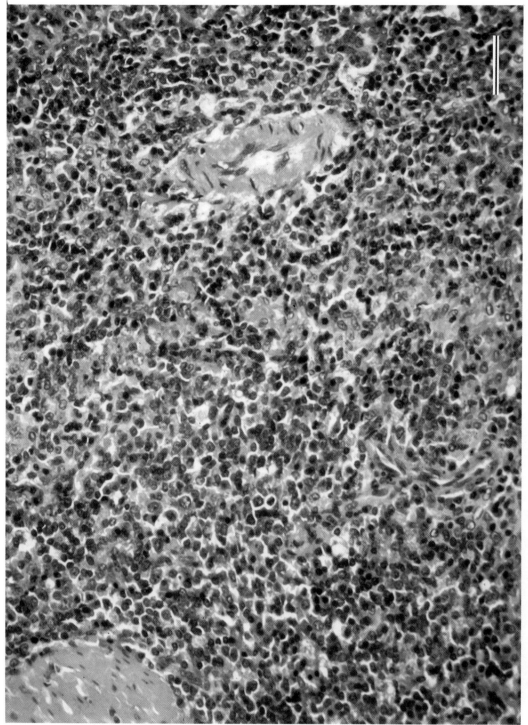

Figure 2.12. **M5a - Monocytic leukemia without maturation.** Spleen section from case shown in Figure 2.10 showing complete replacement of normal tissue with leukemic cells *(H&E). Bar = 40 μm.*

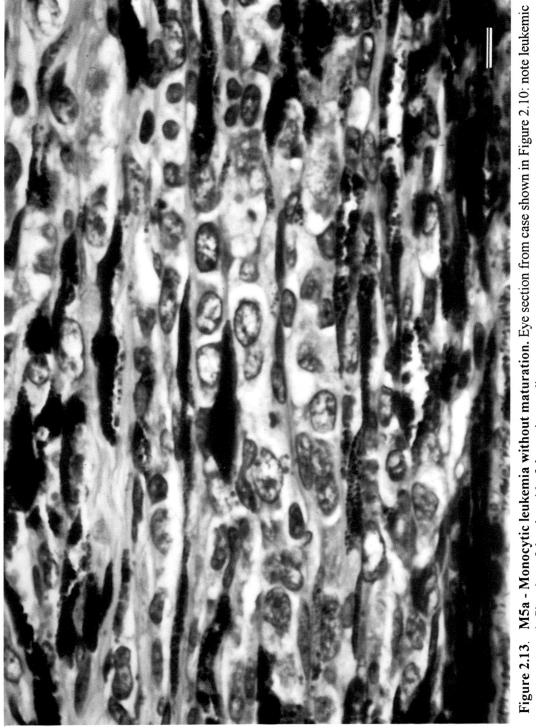

Figure 2.13. **M5a - Monocytic leukemia without maturation.** Eye section from case shown in Figure 2.10: note leukemic infiltration of the choroid of the tunica media *(H&E). Bar = 10 μm. (From Tolle et al. 1982b, p. 246. Courtesy S. Karger AG, Basel).*

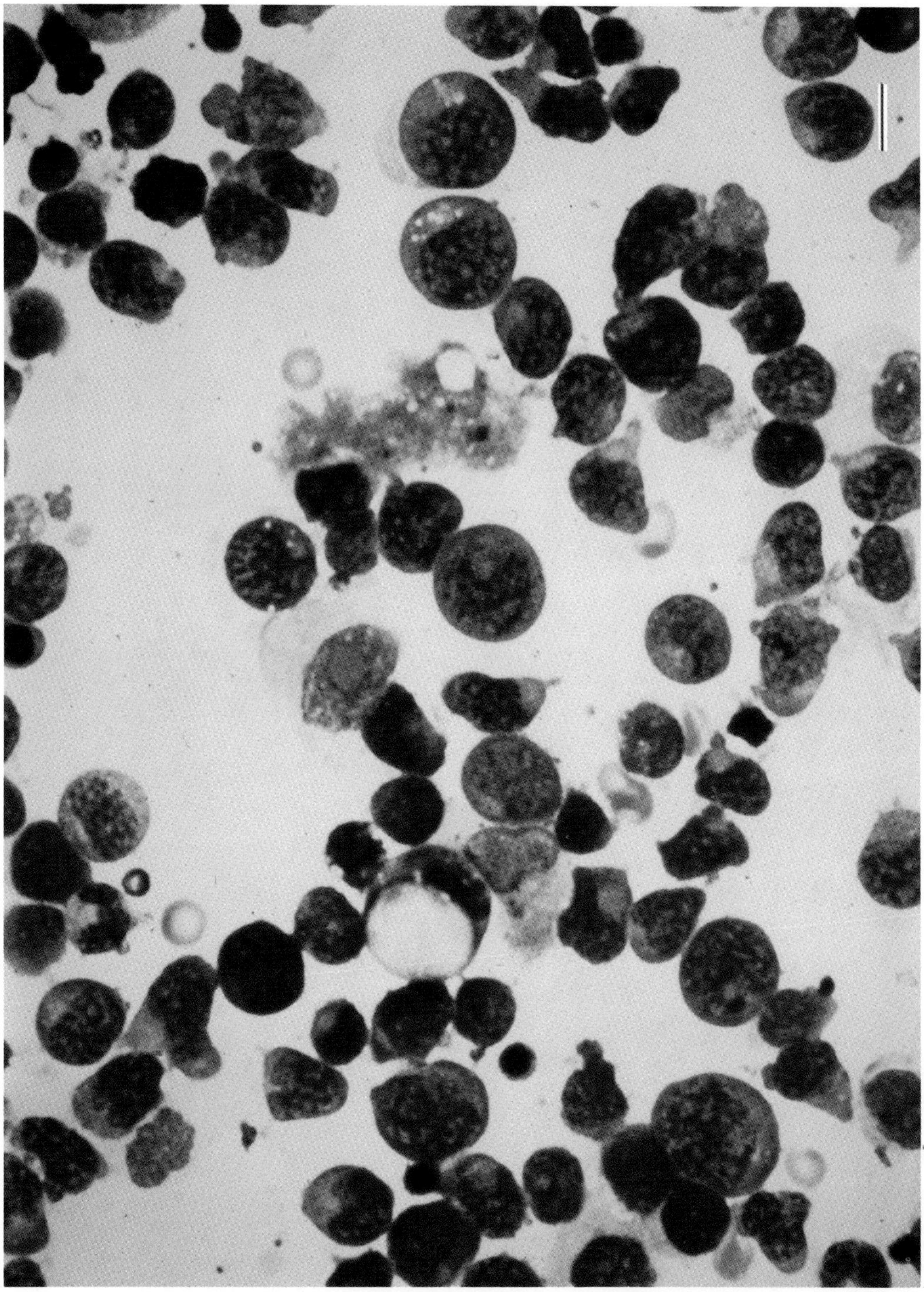

Figure 2.14. **M5a - Monocytic leukemia without maturation.** Terminal bone-marrow aspirate showing a predominance of monoblasts with more condensed chromatin than seen in the blast cells shown in Figures 2.10 and 2.11. Nuclear folding is also more evident in this case *(Dog 1382, W-G). Bar = 10 μm.*

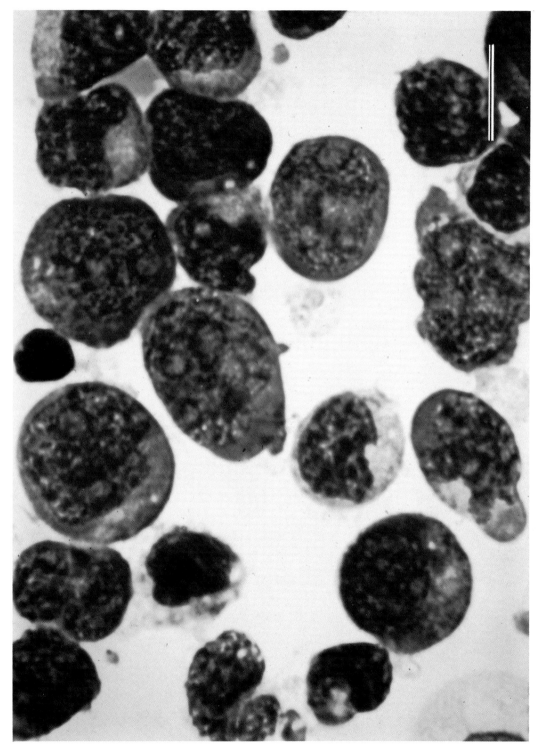

Figure 2.15. M5a - Monocytic leukemia without maturation. Same preparation as in Figure 2.14 at higher magnification. *Bar = 10 μm.*

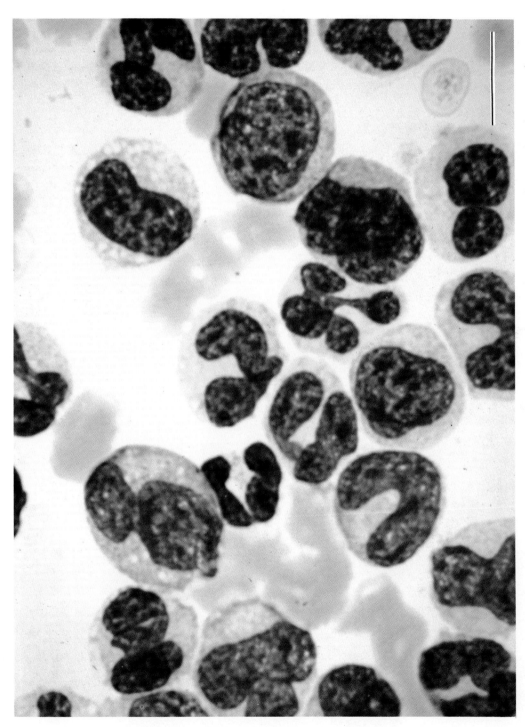

Figure 2.16. **M5b - Monocytic leukemia with maturation.** Terminal peripheral blood buffy coat showing a nearly pure population of monocytes. Note the band and metamyelocyte-like shaped nuclei and ground glass appearance of the cytoplasm *(Dog 2331, W-G). Bar = 10 μm.*

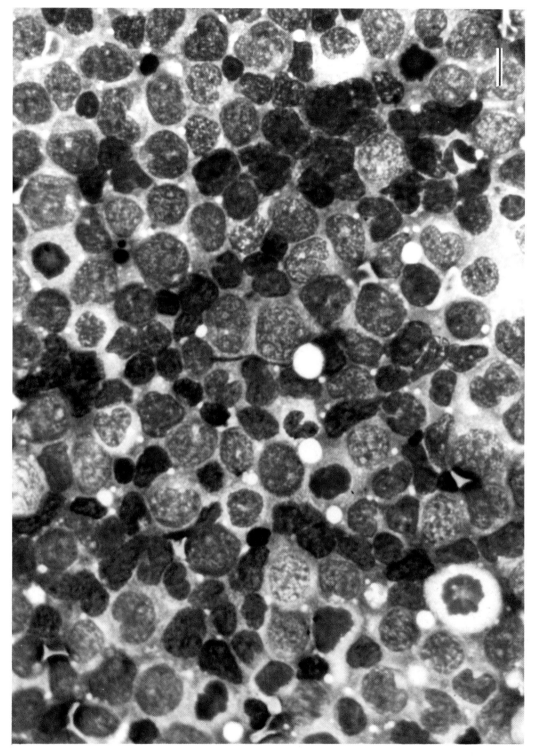

Figure 2.17. M5b - Monocytic leukemia with maturation. Terminal bone-marrow imprint from case shown in Figure 2.16 showing a monoblast/promonocyte hiatus with a paucity of granulocytic and erythroid elements *(W-G). Bar = 10 μm.*

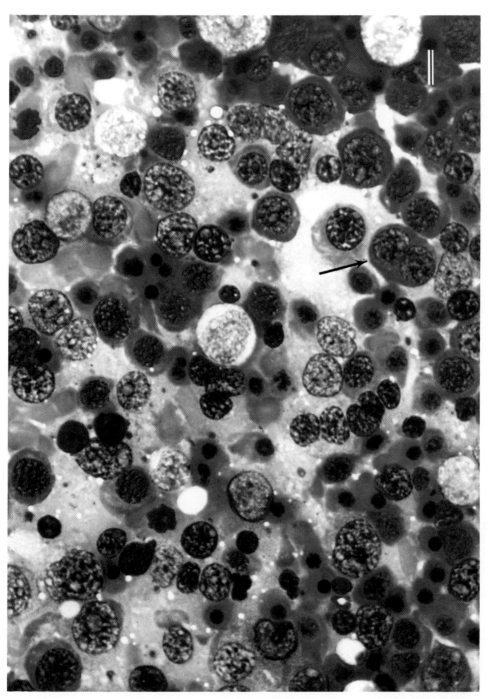

Figure 2.18. **M6 - Erythroleukemia**. Periodic acid Schiff (PAS) stain on terminal bone-marrow imprint showing marked erythroblastic hyperplasia, with a large proportion of cells being rubriblasts. There is a smaller proportion of myeloblasts and myelocytes. Note occasional double-nucleated rubriblasts (→), megaloblastic features, and degree of karyorrhexis in the later erythroblast stages. The erythroblasts are PAS-negative. *(Dog 1366, PAS/W-G). Bar = 10 μm.*

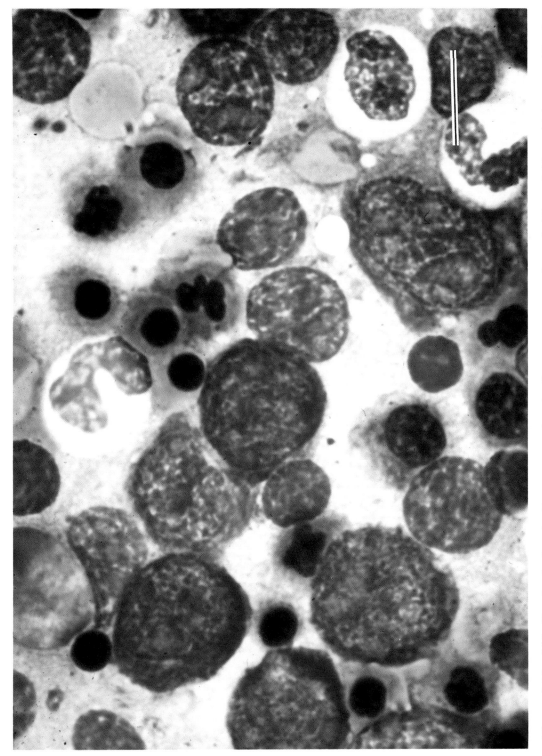

Figure 2.19. **M6 - Erythroleukemia**. Bone-marrow imprint from same case as shown in Figure 2.18 at a higher magnification *(W-G). Bar = 10 μm.*

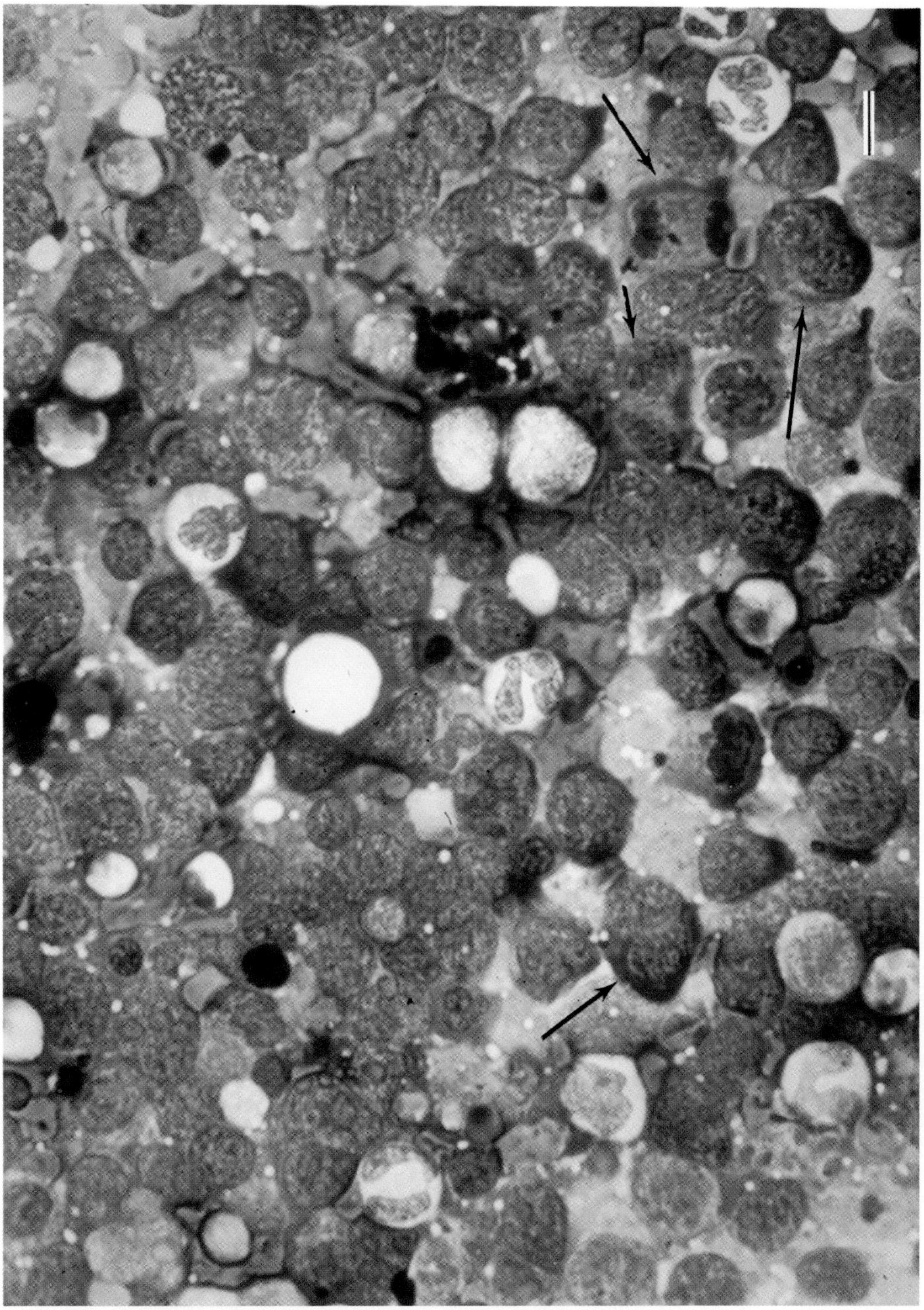

Figure 2.20. **M6 - Erythroleukemia.** Spleen imprint showing a rubriblast hiatus. Many cells are stripped of cytoplasm and appear as naked nuclei. Note occasional double-nucleated forms, mitotic figures (→), and few granulocytes. *(Dog 1469, W-G). Bar = 10 µm. (From Tolle, Fritz, and Norris 1977, p. 509. Courtesy of Harper and Row Publishers, Inc., Philadelphia, PA).*

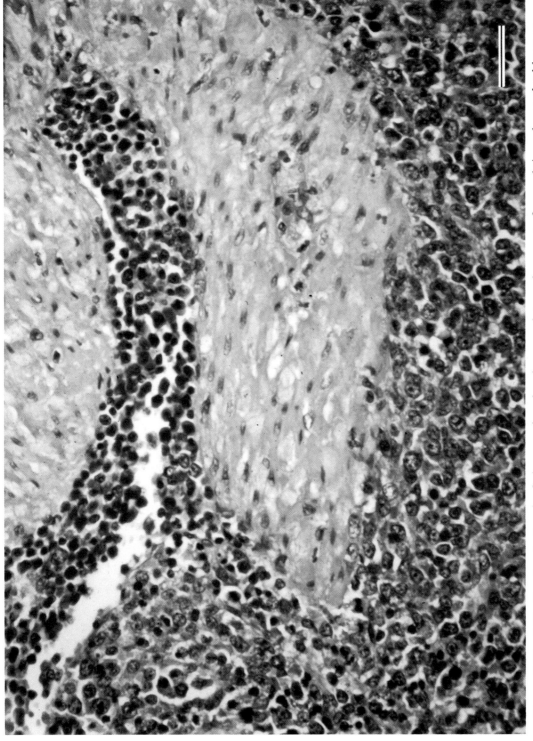

Figure 2.21. **M6 - Erythroleukemia**. Spleen section showing complete replacement of normal tissue by erythroblasts *(Dog 2968, H&E). Bar = 40 μm.*

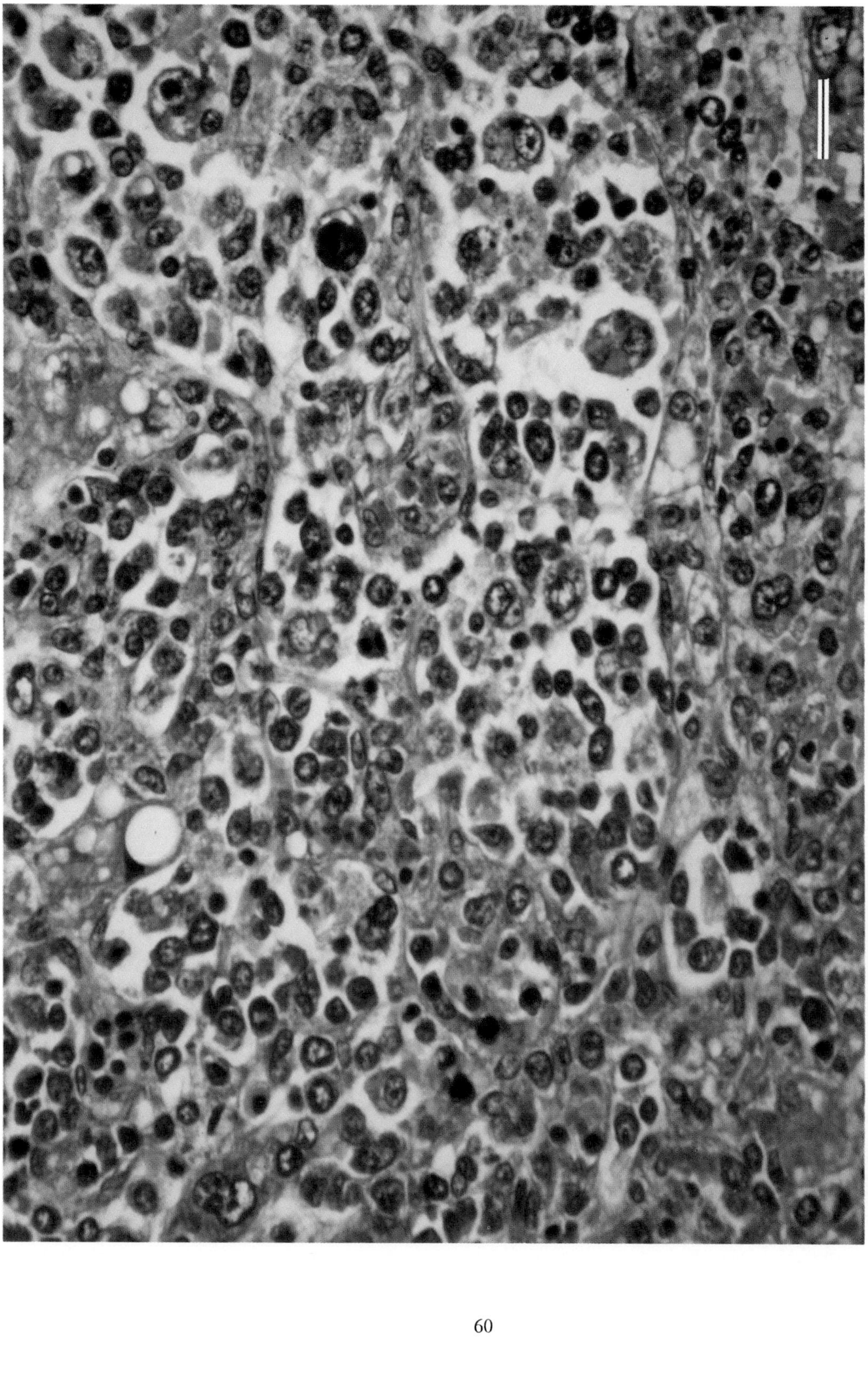

Figure 2.22. M6 - Erythroleukemia. Liver section from case shown in Figure 2.21, showing infiltration by erythroblasts *(H&E). Bar = 20 µm.*

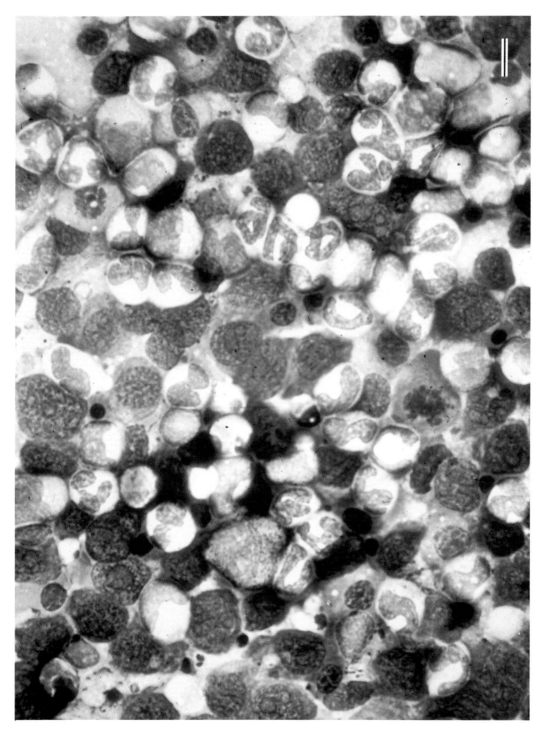

Figure 2.23. **EM - Erythremic myelosis.** Terminal bone-marrow imprint showing severe maturation defect of the erythroid series; the majority of cells are rubriblasts. The granulocytic population appears normal *(Dog 1439, W-G). Bar = 10 μm.*

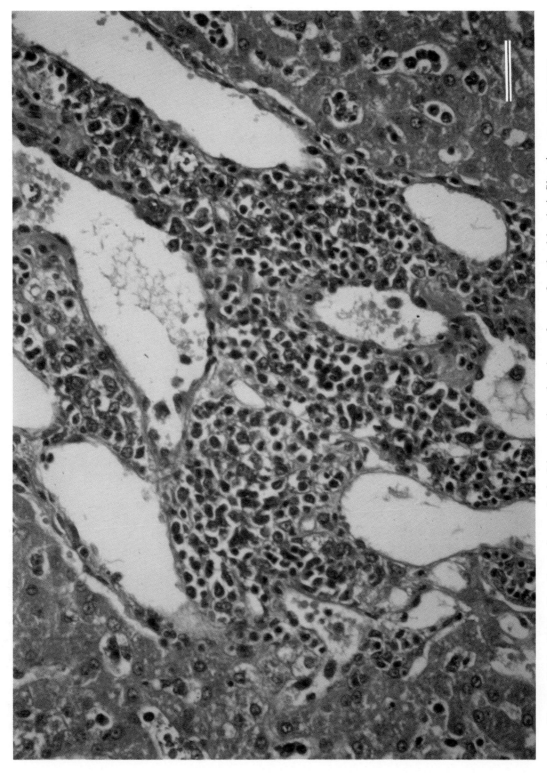

Figure 2.24. **EM - Erythremic myelosis.** Liver section showing a focus of erythroblastic infiltration *(Dog 2976, H&E)*.
Bar = 40 μm.

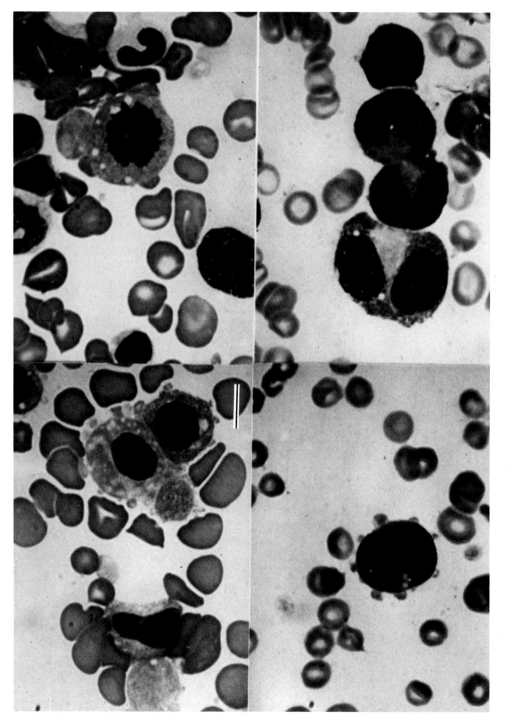

Figure 2.27. M7(b) - Megakaryocytic leukemia with maturation. Peripheral blood buffy coat. Composite of photomicrographs showing various forms of circulating micromegakaryocytes. Note binucleated and mononucleated forms and one cell in mitosis. Also note cytoplasmic buds and giant platelets *(Dog 3255, W-G). Bar = 10 μm for all photomicrographs as shown in composite.*

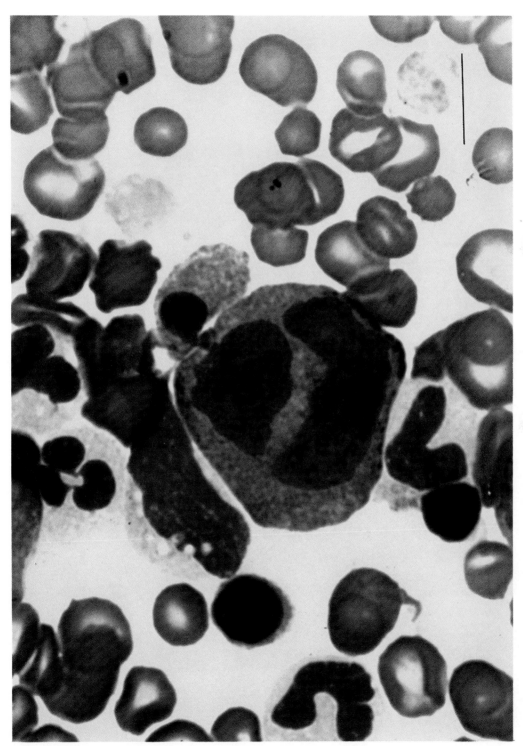

Figure 2.28. **M7(b) - Megakaryocytic leukemia with maturation.** Peripheral blood buffy coat from case shown in Figure 2.27 showing aberrant micromegakaryocyte with attached cytoplasmic fragment containing a portion of nucleus *(W-G). Bar = 10 μm.*

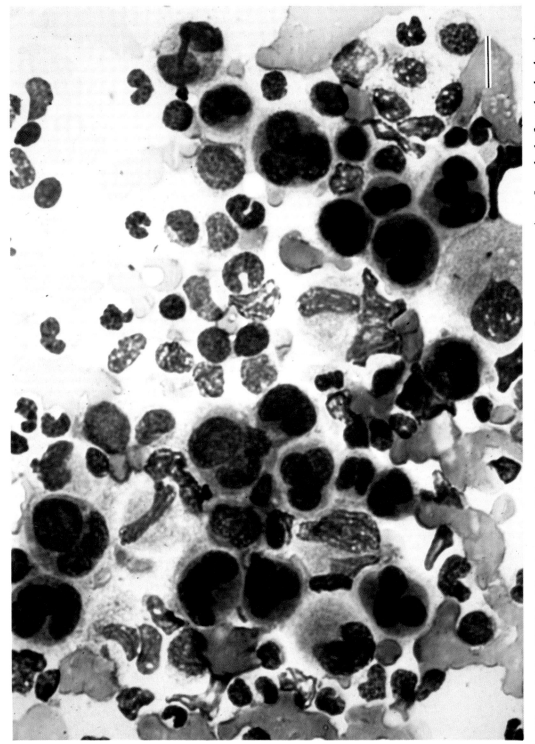

Figure 2.29. M7(b) - Megakaryocytic leukemia with maturation. Bone-marrow aspirate 5 weeks before death, showing clusters of micromegakaryocytes *(Dog 3255, W-G). Bar = 10 μm.*

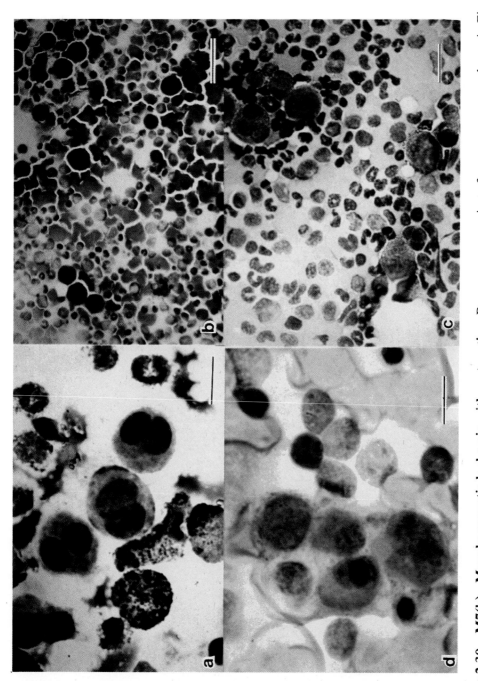

Figure 2.30. M7(b) - **Megakaryocytic leukemia with maturation**. Bone-marrow aspirate from same case as shown in Figure 2.29. Composite of photomicrographs showing cytochemical characteristics of micromegakaryocytes.

a. myeloperoxidase (-)   *(MPO/HH)   Bar = 10 μm.*
b. nonspecific esterase (+)   *(NSE/HH)   Bar = 40 μm.*
c. acetylcholinesterase (+)   *(ACHE/HH) Bar = 20 μm.*
d. periodic-acid Schiff (+)   *(PAS/HH)   Bar = 10 μm.*

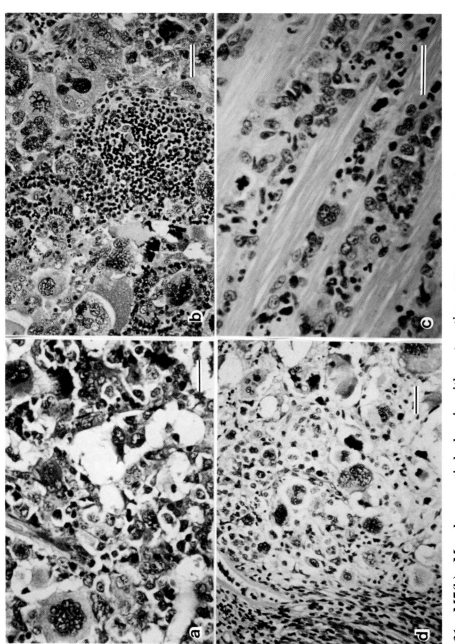

Figure 2.31. M7(b) - Megakaryocytic leukemia with maturation, *(H&E stain, Bar = 40 μm).*

a. Sternal bone-marrow section showing megakaryocytic hyperplasia consisting of aberrant megakaryocytes and micromegakaryocytes *(Dog 390).*

b. Axillary lymph-node section showing marked infiltration with aberrant megakaryocytes and micromegakaryocytes *(Dog 3871).*

c. Section of gluteal muscle showing infiltration with megakaryoblasts and micromegakaryocytes *(Dog 3255).*

d. Section of ovary from same case as shown in Figure 2.31b. Note infiltration with aberrant megakaryocytes.

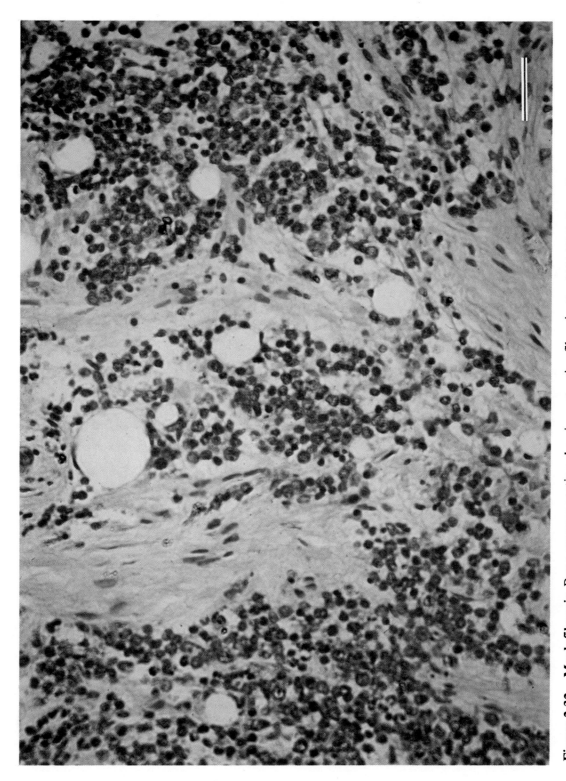

Figure 2.32. Myelofibrosis. Bone-marrow section showing extensive fibrosis *(Dog 3084, H&E). Bar = 40 μm.*

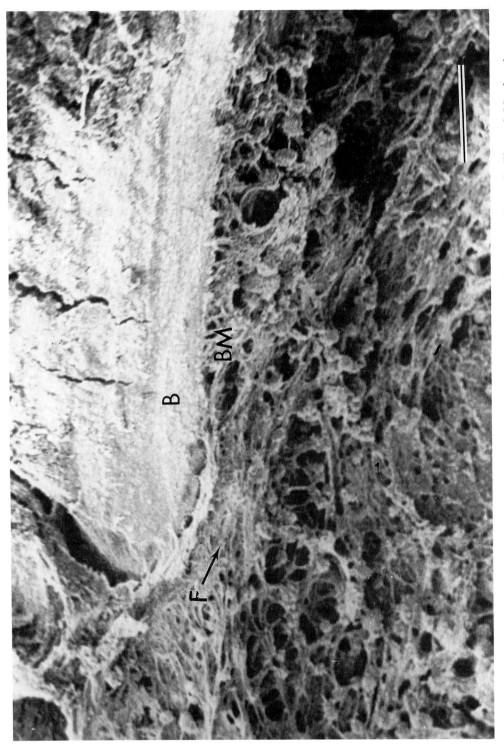

Figure 2.33. **Myelofibrosis.** Scanning electron micrograph of rib bone marrow from case shown in Figure 2.32, showing extensive endosteal fibrosis(F) along the bone (B)/bone marrow (BM) interface. Note the paucity of hematopoietic cells in the parenchyma. *Bar = 50 μm. (From Seed et al. 1982, p. 386. Courtesy Scanning Electron Microscopy, Inc., AMF O'Hare, Chicago, IL).*

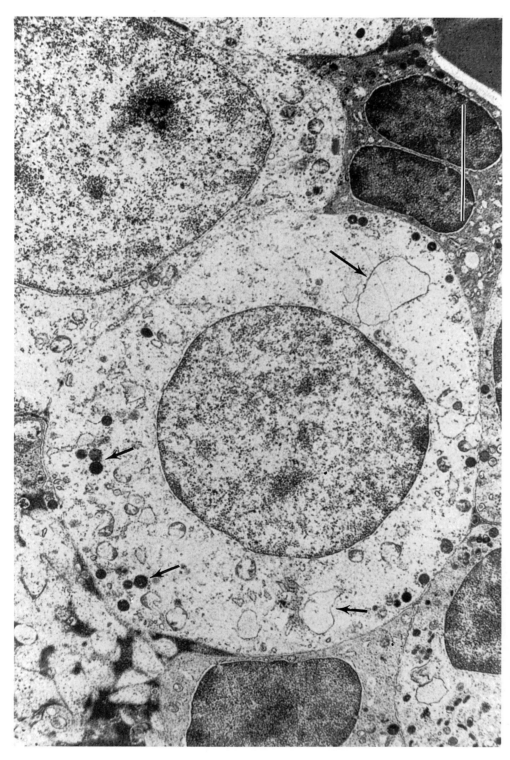

Figure 2.34. M7(b) - Megakaryocytic leukemia with maturation. Transmission electron micrograph of biopsied rib bone marrow, showing micromegakaryocyte. The cytoplasm contains a few dense granules and dilated saccules (→). No evidence of a demarcation membrane system is seen. *Dog 3255, Bar = 10 μm. (From Tolle et al. 1982a, p. 369. Courtesy Scanning Electron Microscopy, Inc., AMF O'Hare, Chicago, IL).*

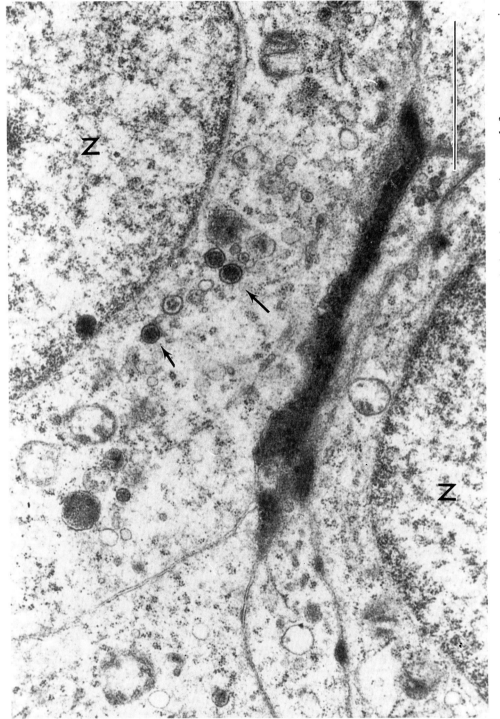

Figure 2.35. **M7(b) - Megakaryocytic leukemia with maturation.** Transmission electron micrograph from same case as in Figure 2.34, showing a portion of two megakaryoblasts. Distinct alpha ("bullseye") granules are seen in the cytoplasm (→). The nuclei (N) are very immature. *Bar = 5 μm. (From Tolle et al. 1982a, p. 369, Courtesy Scanning Electron Microscopy, Inc., AMF O'Hare, Chicago, IL).*

CHAPTER 3: Tumors of the Liver

Glenn N. Taylor
University of Utah

INTRODUCTION

The nomenclature of the liver tumors presented in this fascicle was based on the World Health Organization's International Histological Classification of Tumors of Domestic Animals (Ponomarkov and Mackey 1976). The scope of the observations was limited principally to those observed in beagles with variable burdens of ^{293}Pu or ^{241}Am. The nomenclature of these lesions is shown in Table 3.1, with an index to illustrations and corresponding SNOMED database codes.

The liver is an important deposition site in dogs for these and some of the other actinide elements translocating from the lungs and from wounds, etc., via the blood vascular system (Mays et al. 1970; Stover, Stevens, and Bruenger 1972; and Taylor et al. 1986). It is also well established that hepatic tissue in humans is also a prime deposition site for some of these radionuclides (Magno, Kauffman, and Groulx 1967; McInroy 1976; Rowland and Durbin 1976; Wegener and Hasenohrl 1983). In beagles, the early deposition pattern was initially quite uniform within the hepatic epithelium, but at later times after injection the translocation of a significant portion of the burden to the Kupffer cells, and ultimately to the central and periportal regions, occurred. Focal nodular hyperplasia was also a significant factor in the intrahepatic distribution. The affinity of the beagle liver for these elements makes it one of the prime target organs in the toxicity schemes of ^{239}Pu, ^{241}Am, and some of the other actinides and is one of the major reasons for including the liver in this atlas.

Most of the hyperplastic and the neoplastic lesions that are presented also occur "spontaneously" and are not unique to a radiation etiology. Nevertheless, the dose-response relationships indicated that most of the tumors presented here were radiation-induced.

Injected dosages have been indicated for each respective animal in microocuries per kilogram of body weights, but this is not meant to imply a relationship between a given dose and a given tumor type. For example, some of the specific tumors were observed over a wide spectrum of treatment levels.

It should also be noted that this chapter presents only the primary hepatic tumors that have been observed, to date, in beagle studies at several DOE laboratories. Thus, additions to this chapter will probably be necessary as data are received from experiments that are still in progress or that are being conducted in other facilities.

Table 3.1. Liver Neoplasia Nomenclature, Index of Figures, and SNODOG Database Codes.

Nomenclature	Figure(s)	SNODOG Morphology Code[a]
Non-neoplastic		
Atrophy	3.1	M580000
Nodular hyperplasia	3.2–5	M720300
Neoplastic		
Benign intrahepatic cystadenoma	3.6	M844000
Intrahepatic bile duct adenoma	3.7–9	M816000
Hepatic cell carcinoma	3.10–11	M817030
Intrahepatic cholangiocarcinoma	3.12–15	M816030
Mesothelioma	3.16–17	M905030
Intrahepatic carcinoid	3.18	M824030
Hemangiosarcoma	3.19	M912030
Intrahepatic fibrosarcoma	3.20	M881030
Myxoma	3.21	M884000
Myxosarcoma	3.22	M884030
Mast cell sarcoma	3.23	M974030

[a] Identical to SNOMED, with addition of shaded 6th digit specific to lifespan beagle studies.

REFERENCES

Magno, P. J., P. E. Kauffman, and P. R. Groulx. 1967. Plutonium in environmental and biological media. Health Phys. 13:1325-1330.

Mays, C. W., G. N. Taylor, W. S. S. Jee, and T. F. Doughtery. 1970. Speculated risk to bone and liver from ^{239}Pu. Health Phys. 19:601-610.

McInroy, J. F. 1976. The Los Alamos Scientific Laboratory's Human Autopsy Tissue Study, pp. 249-270. In: *The Health Effects of Plutonium and Radium*, W. S. S. Jee, Ed. J. W. Press, Salt Lake City, UT.

Ponomarkov, V. and L. J. Mackey. 1976. XIII. Tumours of the Liver and Biliary System, pp. 187-194. In: *The Bulletin of the World Health Organization*, International Histological Classification of Tumours of Domestic Animals, 53, No. 2-3, WHO, Geneva, Switzerland.

Rowland, R. E., and P. W. Durbin. 1976. Survival, Causes of Death, and Estimated Tissue Doses in a Group of Human Beings Injected with Plutonium. pp. 329-342. In: *The Health Effects of Plutonium and Radium*, W. S. S. Jee, Ed. J. W. Press, Salt Lake City, UT.

Selye, H., 1965. *The Mast Cells*, p. 91. Baltimore, Waverly Press, Inc., MD.

Stover, B. J., W. Stevens, and F. W. Bruenger. Chemical Associations of ^{239}Pu(IV) and ^{241}Am(III) in Blood, Liver, and Thyroid, pp. 129-169. In: *Radiobiology of Plutonium*, B. J. Stover and W. S. S. Jee, Eds. The J. W. Press, Salt Lake City, UT.

Taylor, G. N., C. W. Mays, M. E. Wrenn, L. Shabestari, and R. D. Lloyd. 1986. Incidence of Liver Tumors in Beagles with Body Burdens of ^{239}Pu or ^{241}Am, pp. 268-285. In: *Life-Span Radiation Effects Studies in Animals: What Can They Tell Us?* R. C. Thompson and J. A. Mahaffy, Eds. CONF 830951, NTIS, Springfield, VA.

Wegener, K. and K Hasenohrl. 1983. Recent results of the German Thorotrast study: Pathoanatomical changes in animal experiments and comparison to human thorotrastosis. *Health Phys*. 44 (Suppl. 1): 307-316.

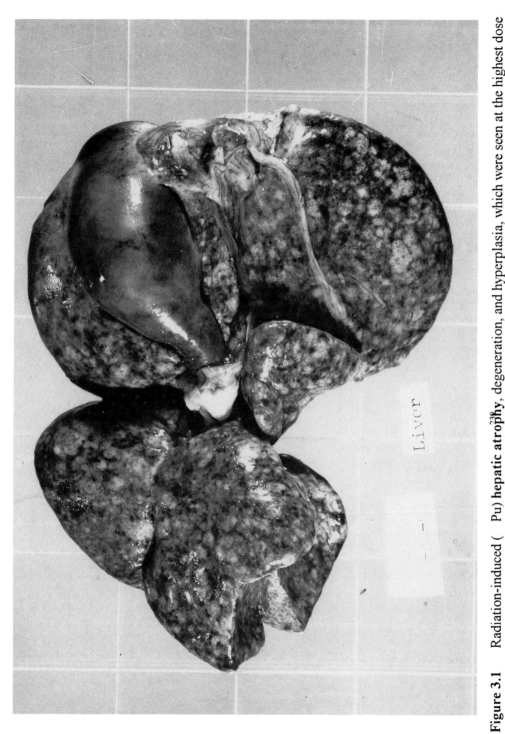

Figure 3.1 Radiation-induced (^{239}Pu) **hepatic atrophy**, degeneration, and hyperplasia, which were seen at the highest dose level studied (3 μCi/kg). Although significant hepatocyte hyperplasia was present in this liver, the replacement of the parenchyma did not keep pace with necrosis, and the mass of this liver was about one-third of normal. Also, the normal sinusoidal architecture was not maintained in the regenerated tissue, producing marked portal hypertension and ascites. *Beagle: T46P5 (Male); Age: 3.15 y; Time after injection: 2.01 y; Treatment:3.01 μCi ^{239}Pu/kg.*

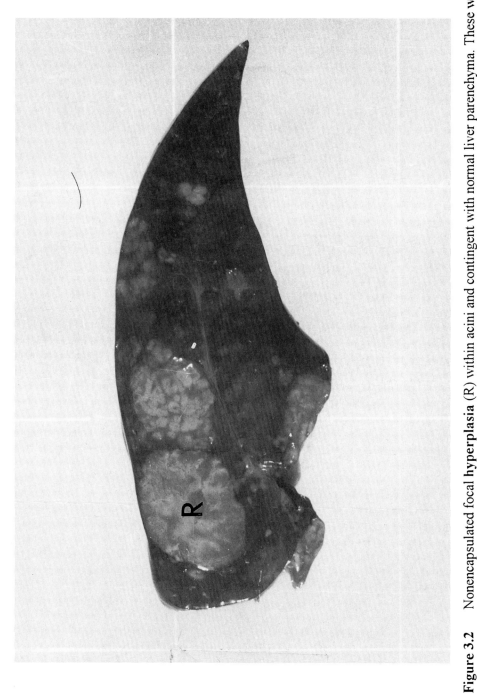

Figure 3.2 Nonencapsulated focal hyperplasia (R) within acini and contingent with normal liver parenchyma. These were subunits of a grossly apparent nodule, shown in Figure 3.2. Such focal hyperplasia produced distortion and enlargement of the involved acini, but the general acinar pattern was usually retained, distinguishing such hyperplasia from hepatic cell adenomas. Although not definitely established, there was evidence that clusters of hyperplastic acini tended to be oriented around a given branch of the portal tree, producing the much larger grossly apparent nodule. Fibrosis was generally not present. *Beagle: F9P1.7 (Female); Age: 8.92 y; Time after injection: 6.85 y; Treatment: 0.0485 μCi* ^{239}*Pu/kg*

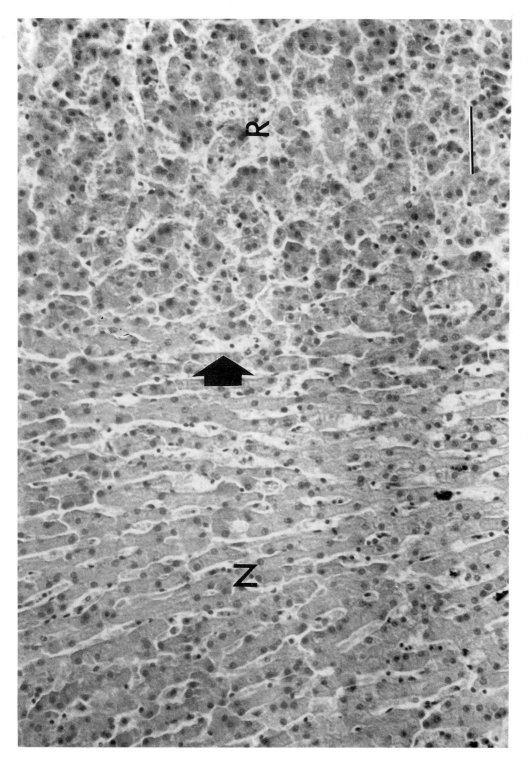

Figure 3.3. Nodular hyperplasia of hepatocytes (R) with atypical arrangement of sinusoids; cords of two or more cells thickness (→); complete absence of encapsulation or separation from the nonhyperplastic hepatocytes (N). *H&E stain. Bar = 60 µm.. Beagle: F2P1 (Female); Age: 14.33 y; Time after injection: 13.18 y; Treatment: 0.0163 µCi ²³⁹Pu/kg, citrate, i.v.*

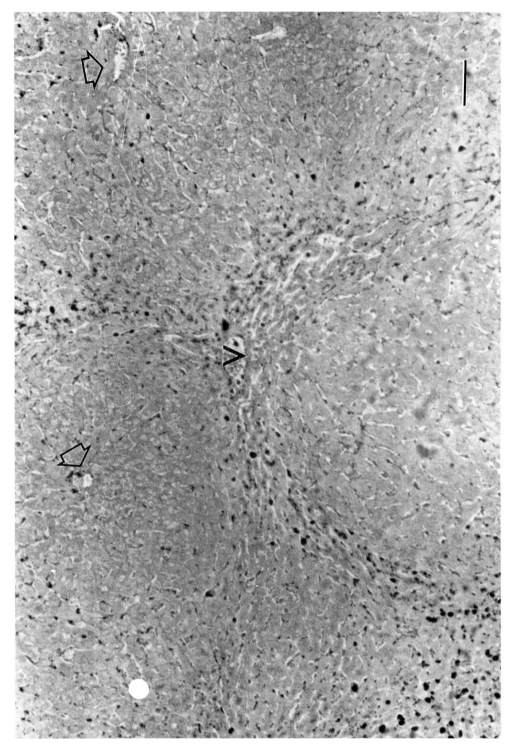

Figure 3.4 Hyperplasia of hepatocytes; expansion appears to arise from the periportal regions of the acini (→) and gives the appearance of reverse lobulation; the residual nonhyperplastic tissue is compressed into the central regions (V). The dark-staining cells, located principally in the central regions, are iron-laden macrophages. *Turnbull blue stain. Bar = 60 μm. Beagle: F2P5 (Female) Age: 7.5 y Time after injection: 4.3 y Treatment: 3.30 μCi ^{239}Pu/kg.*

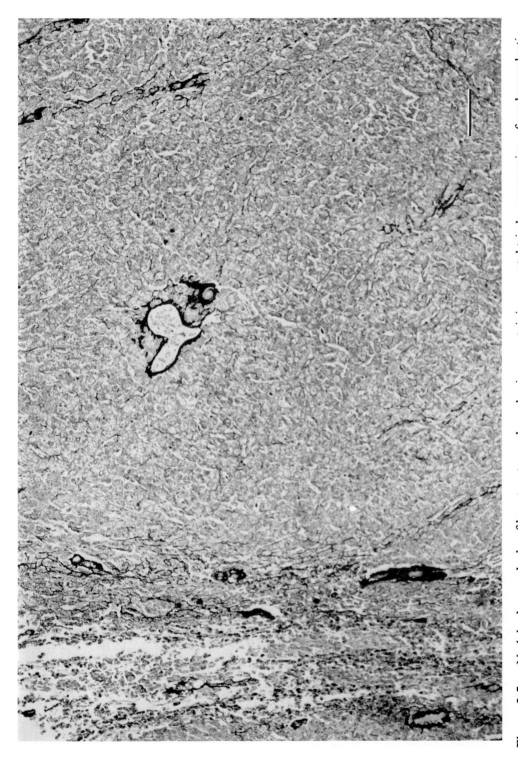

Figure 3.5 Nodular hyperplasia of hepatocytes; enlarged acinus containing a portal triad; compression of nonhyperplastic hepatocytes at the periphery; deficiency of argyrophilic fibers; hepatic cords generally two cells or more in thickness and of atypical arrangement; absence of encapsulation. *Nasser stain. Bar = 60 μm. Beagle: M3P1.7 (Female) Age: 11.2 y Time after injection: 9.4 y Treatment: 0.0495 μCi ^{239}Pu/kg.*

82

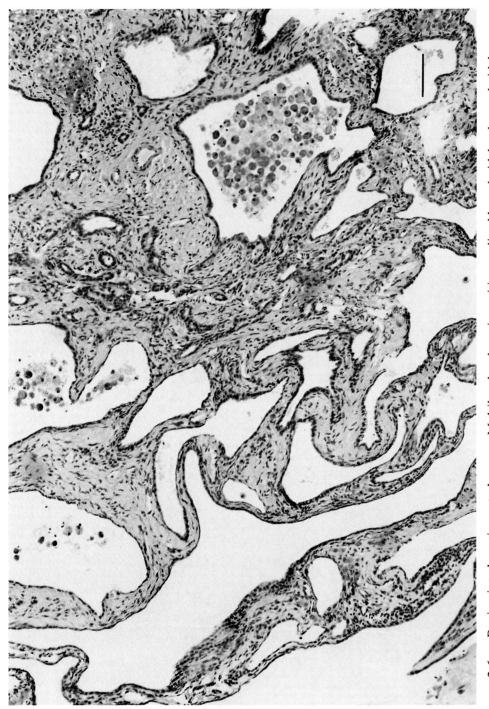

Figure 3.6   Benign intrahepatic cystadenoma. Multiloculated cystic cavities are lined by cuboidal to low-cuboidal epithelium and contain watery or mucinous exudate with monocytic infiltrates. In some instances the individual compartments vary in size from less than 1 mm to over 10 cm in diameter. The fibrous stroma is abundant and is focally infiltrated with leukocytes. Mitotic figures were not seen. *H&E stain. Bar = 60 μm. Beagle: F101P0.5Y (Female) Age: 11.8 y Time after injection: 11.5 y Treatment: 0.00617 μCi ²³⁹Pu/kg.*

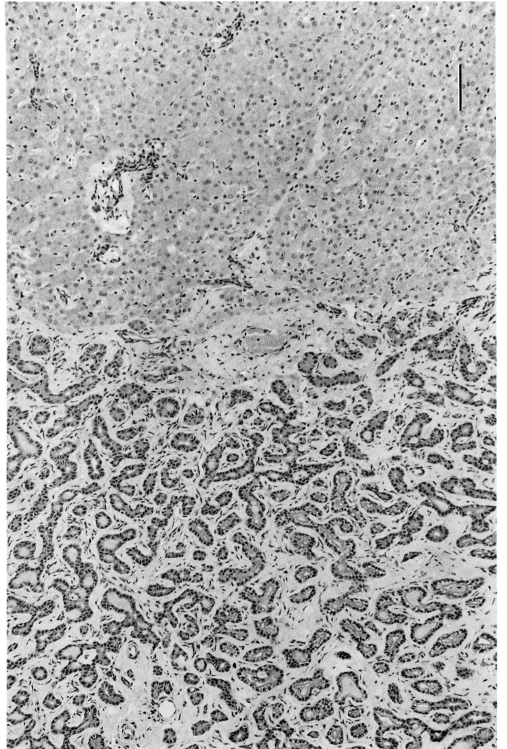

Figure 3.7 Larger intrahepatic bile duct adenoma; no cystic change; ductules are lined with regular cubodial epithelium; only moderate degree of interductular fibrosis; absence of pseudocapsule; tumors of this phenotype appeared to be slow growing and were never observed to metastasize. *H&E stain. Bar = 60 μm. Beagle: M508P2+ (Male) Age: 11.6 y Time after injection: 6.6 y Treatment: 0.0917 μCi 239Pu/kg.*

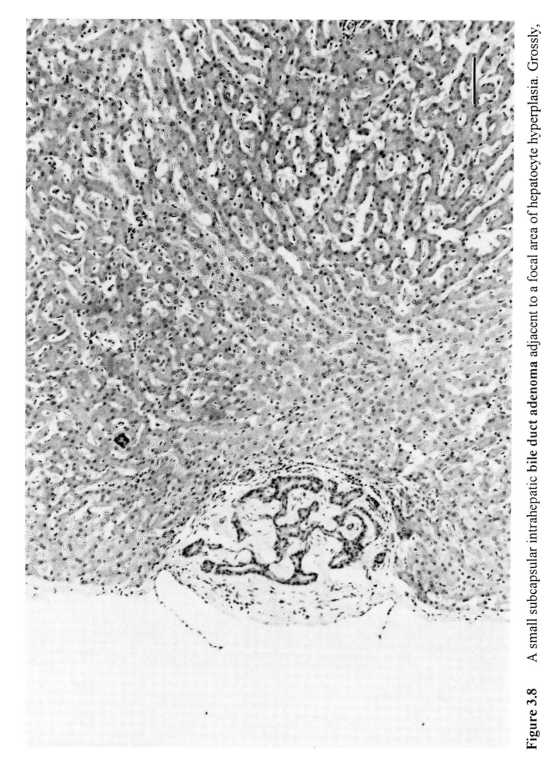

Figure 3.8   A small subcapsular intrahepatic **bile duct adenoma** adjacent to a focal area of hepatocyte hyperplasia. Grossly, it appeared as a small, pale gray focus and was an incidental finding. The glandular structures resemble bile ductules and are lined with cuboidal epithelium. Mitoses were not seen, and the fibrous stroma is abundant. *H&E stain. Bar = 60 µm. Beagle:F44P0.7 (Female) Age: 13.2 y Time after injection: 11.74 y Treatment: 0.0105 µCi ²³⁹Pu/kg.*

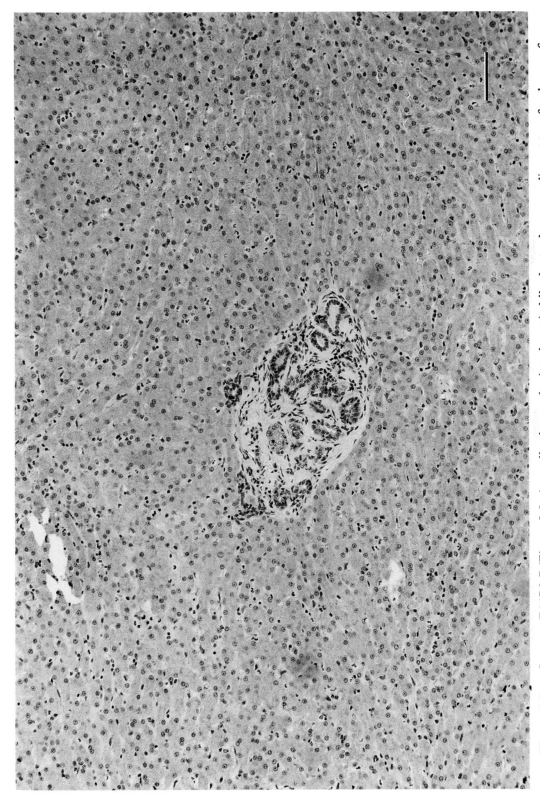

Figure 3.9 Same as F44P0.7 (Figure 3.8.) except for midzonal location. A small subcapsular intrahepatic **bile duct adenoma** adjacent to a focal area of hepatocyte hyperplasia.) *Bar = 60 μm. Beagle: F508P2+ (Female) Age: 11.6 y Time after injection: 6.6 y Treatment: 0.917 μCi* ^{239}*Pu/kg.*

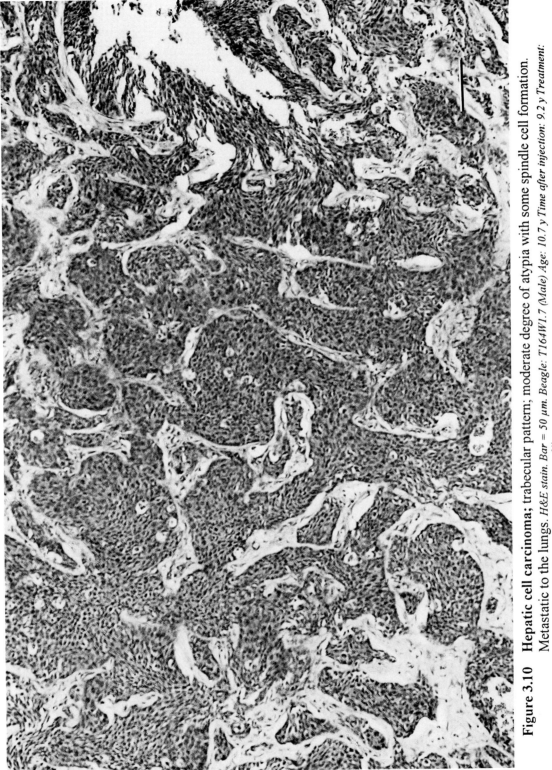

Figure 3.10 Hepatic cell carcinoma; trabecular pattern; moderate degree of atypia with some spindle cell formation. Metastatic to the lungs. *H&E stain. Bar = 50 µm. Beagle: T164W1.7 (Male) Age: 10.7 y Time after injection: 9.2 y Treatment: 0.0481 µCi [241] Am/kg i.v.*

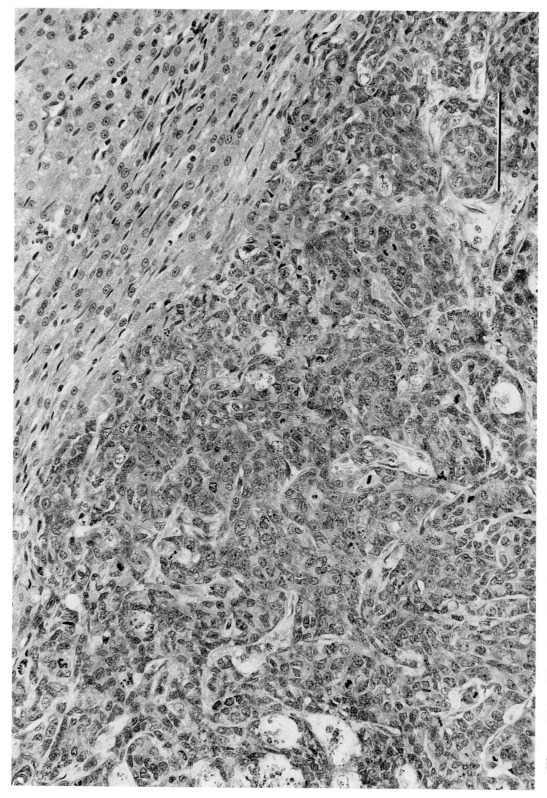

Figure 3.11 **Hepatic cell carcinoma**; trabecular pattern; nonencapsulated; numerous mitoses; significant nuclear atypia. *H&E stain. Bar = 50 µm. Beagle: T164W1.7 (Higher magnification of same tumor as in Figure 3.10)*

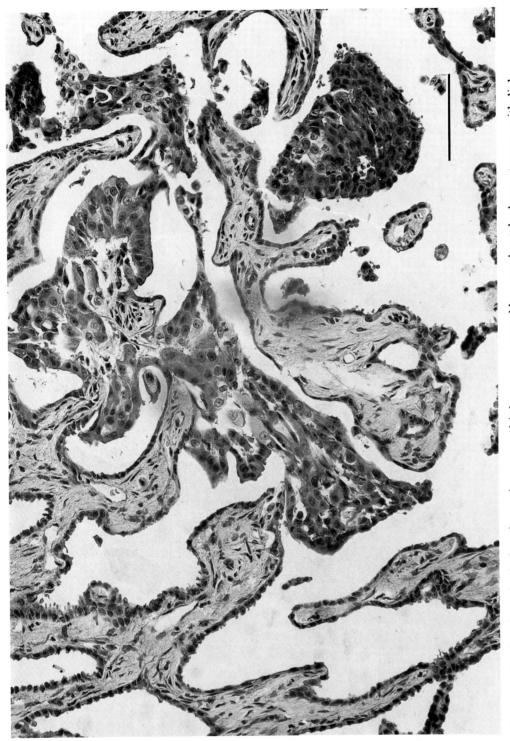

Figure 3.12 Intrahepatic cholangiocarcinoma; multiple cysts separated by a moderately dense stroma; epithelial pleomorphism evident in both the lining of the cystic cavities and the papillary projections; neoplastic epithelium varies from low cuboidal to tall columnar; complete loss of polarity in some regions. *H&E stain. Bar = 60 µm. Beagle: T164W1.7 (Male) Age: 10.7 y Time after injection: 9.2 years Treatment: 0.0481 µCi²⁴¹Am/kg i.v.*

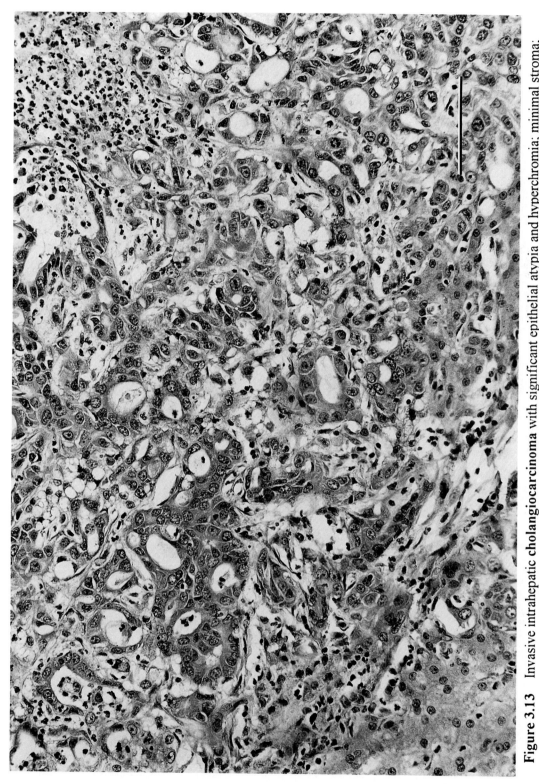

Figure 3.13 Invasive intrahepatic cholangiocarcinoma with significant epithelial atypia and hyperchromia; minimal stroma; irregular ductule formation; and focal leukocytic infiltrates. *H&E stain. Bar = 60 μm. Beagle: T167W1.7 (Female) Age: 10.6 y Time after injection: 9.2 y Treatment: 0.0482 μCi ^{241}Am/kg i.v.*

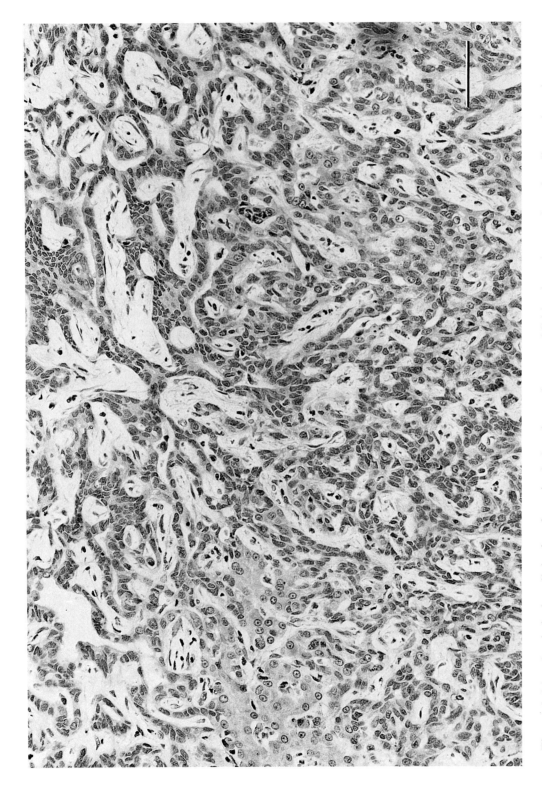

Figure 3.14 A relatively cellular intrahepatic cholangiocarcinoma exhibiting invasiveness into the adjacent hepatic parenchyma; epithelium varying from low cubodial to tall columnar; a relatively fine stroma. *H&E stain. Bar = 60 μm Beagle: M125W1.7 (Male) Age: 11.3 y Time after injection: 9.9 y Treatment: 0.0471 μCi ^{241}Am/kg i.v.*

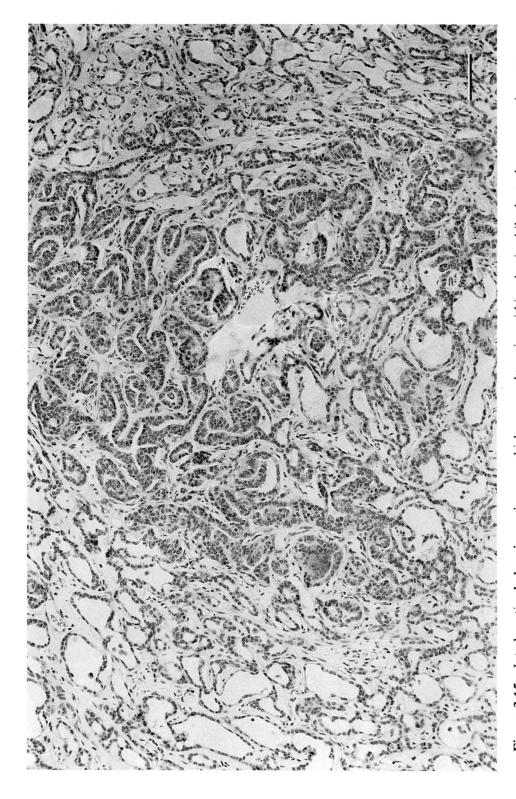

Figure 3.15   Intrahepatic cholangiocarcinoma, which appeared to arise within a benign bile-duct adenoma; carcinomatous transition characterized by: epithelial elements, which are frequently several cells in thickness, and which, in some instances, occlude the lumina; enlarged pleomorphic nuclei; papilla-like projections extending into the lumina; increased numbers of mitotic figures. *H&E stain. Bar = 60 µm. Beagle: F106P1.7Y (Female) Age: 10.9 y Time after injection: 10.6 y Treatment: 0.0529 µCi ²³⁹Pu/kg i.v.*

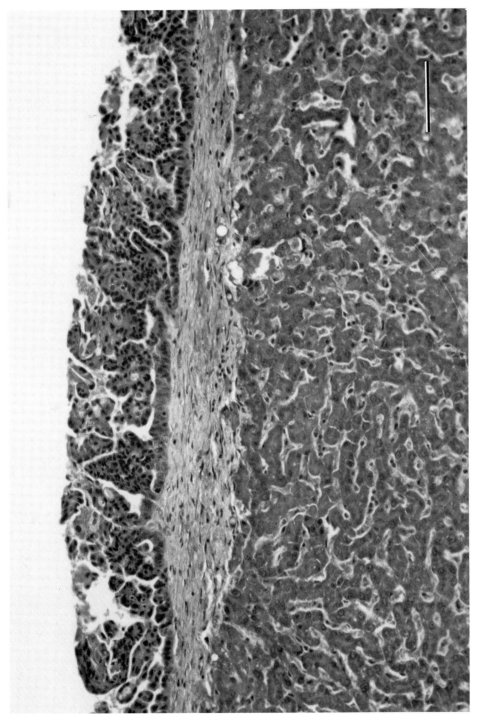

Figure 3.16 Mesothelioma (malignant), which appeared to arise from the serous surface of the liver; multiple gland-like papilla projecting above the capsule; general epithelioid appearance; some solid nests of cells; underlying liver capsule thickened. (Mesothelial lining of the liver is within alpha-particle range of subcapsular deposits in animal with normal capsular thickness.) *H&E stain. Bar = 60 μm. Beagle: M35W4 (Male) Age: 4.9 y Time after injection: 4.2 y Treatment: 0.902 μCi²⁴¹Am/kg i.v.*

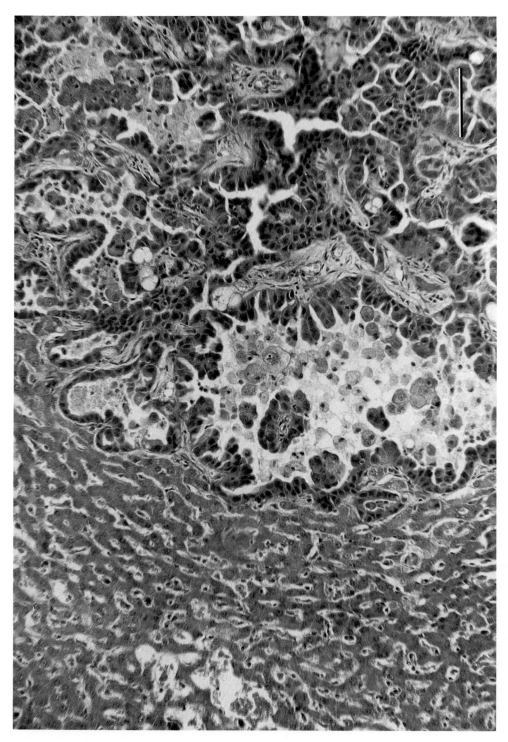

Figure 3.17 Mesothelioma (same dog as in Figure 3.16) showing extensions into hepatic parenchyma and additional detail of the tumor, including the formation of cysts with epithelioid features and exfoliation of individual or clusters of cells into such cavities. *H&E stain. Bar = 60 µm. Beagle: M35W4 (Male) Age: 4.9 y Time after injection: 4.2 y Treatment: 0.902 µCi [241] Am/kg i.v.*

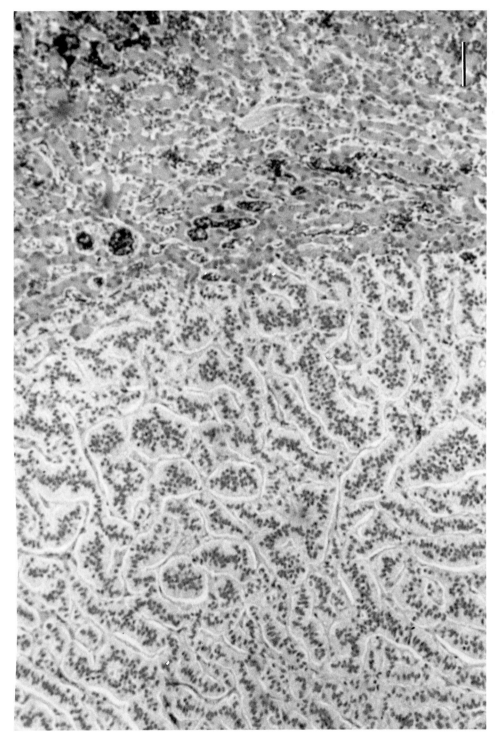

Figure 3.18 Intrahepatic carcinoid; orientation of tall columnar cells toward basement membrane of regularly arranged papillae. (NOTE: The diagnosis was established by immunohistochemistry.) Cytoplasmic granules could not be demonstrated by the Grimelius stain. *H&E stain. Bar = 60 μm. Beagle: 854B Age:10.5 y Time after exposure: 9.4 y Treatment:$^{239}PuO_2$ monodisperse aerosol; initial lung burden: 0.7 μCi/kg.*

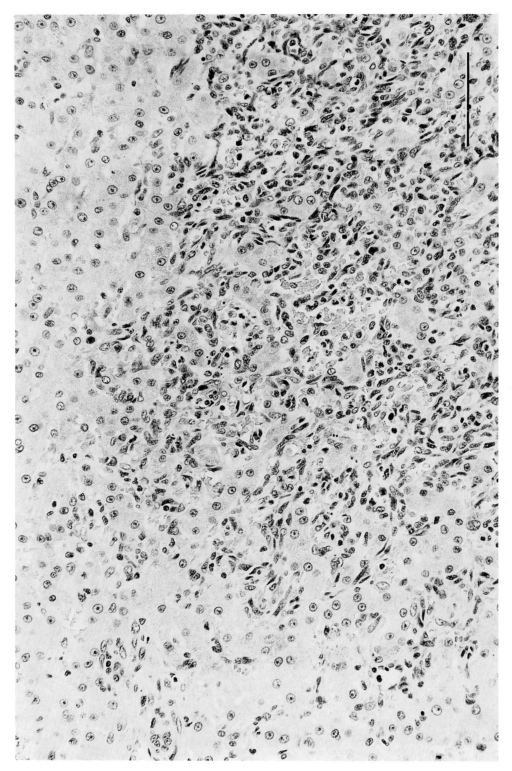

Figure 3.19 Hemangiosarcoma, which arose within the liver. Spindle-shaped atypical cells with enlarged hyperchromatic nuclei have formed vascular channels; malignant cells have displaced or are overlying the sinusoidal cells. A tendency to line and spread along the sinusoids is evident. *H&E stain. Bar = 60 μm. Beagle: M125W1.7 (Male) Age: 11.3 y Time after injection: 9.9 y Treatment: 0.0471 μCi ²⁴¹Am/kg i.v.*

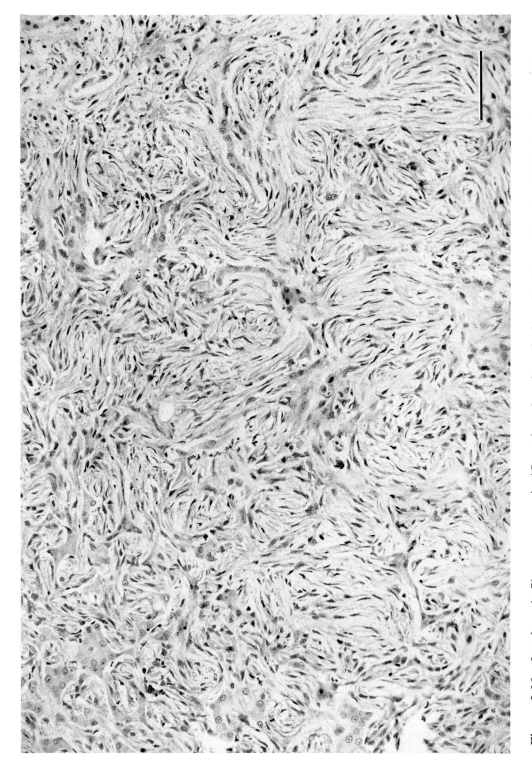

Figure 3.20   Intrahepatic **fibrosarcoma**; significant invasion along the hepatic plates and scattered islands of entrapped hepatocytes; abnormal mitotic index; whorled arrangement of fibroblasts. *H&E stain. Bar = 60 μm. Beagle: M140W1.7 (Male) Age: 8.8 y Time after injection: 7.4 y Treatment: 0.0469 μCi ²⁴¹Am/kg i.v.*

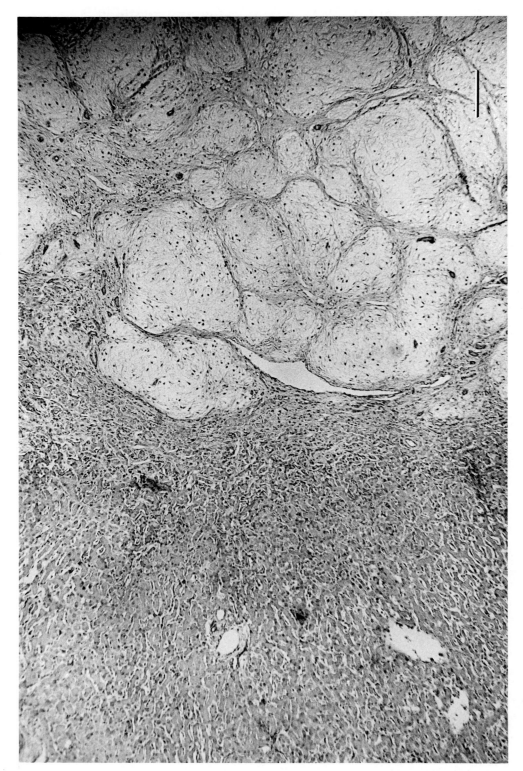

Figure 3.21 **Myxoma**; sparsely cellular; abundant mucin; compression of the surrounding hepatic parenchyma; minor bile-duct hyperplasia; entrapment of some ducts within the stromal regions. Mitotic figures were not seen. *H&E stain. Bar = 15 μm. Beagle: M20W1 (Male) Age: 9.8 y Time after injection: 8.4 y Treatment: 0.016 μCi* [241] *Am/kg i.v.*

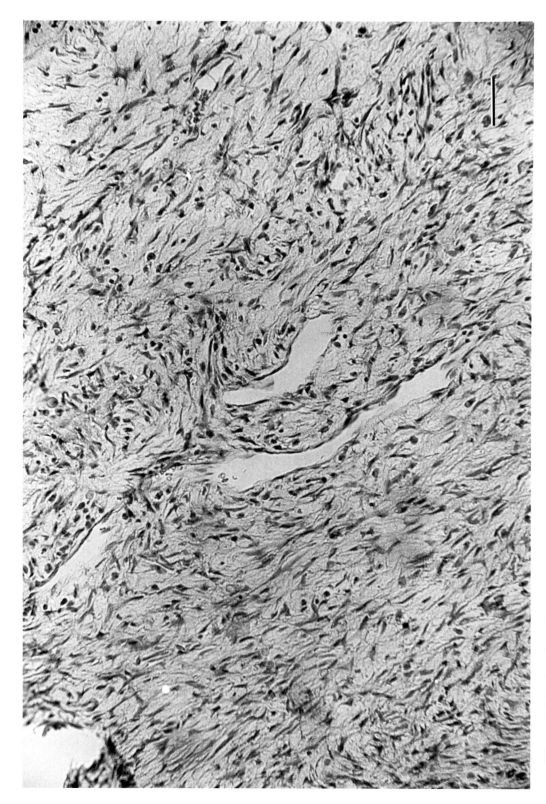

Figure 3.22　Intrahepatic myxosarcoma; moderate mucin; occasional mitoses; increased cellularity with spindle or stellate-type cells. *H&E stain. Bar = 60 μm. Beagle: M20W1 (Male) Age: 9.8 y Time after injection: 8.4 y Treatment: 0.016 μCi ^{24U}Am/kg i.v.*

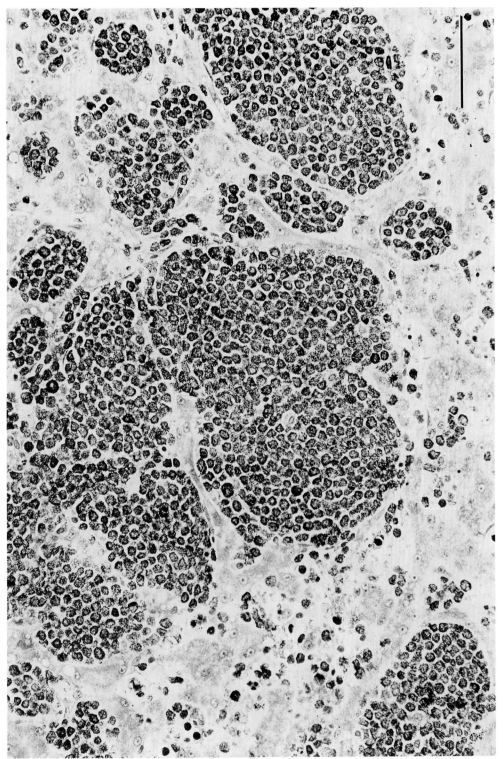

Figure 3.23 **Mast cell sarcoma**, which arose within the liver; multiple colonies of cells with Giemsa-positive cytoplasmic granules. It should be noted that the dog normally has a moderate number of mast cells in hepatic tissue (Selye 1965). Mast cell tumors in the skin, intestine, etc. of this dog were not observed. *Giemsa stain. Bar = 60 μm. Beagle: M27W2 (Male) Age: 9.2 y Time after injection: 7.9 y Treatment: 0.0961 μCi ²⁴¹Am/kg i.v.*

CHAPTER 4: Tumors of the Lung

Gerald E. Dagle
Pacific Northwest National Laboratory
Currently at Washington State University—Tri Cities

Fletcher F. Hahn
Inhalation Toxicology Research Institute

INTRODUCTION

The classification of lung tumors follows a modification of a nomenclature proposed by the World Health Organization (World Health Organization 1974) that is similar to other classification schemes (Moulton 1978; Moulton, von Tscharner, and Schneider 1981). The nomenclature emphasizes the histologic patterns rather than the site of origin of the tumors. Diagnoses were made from paraffin sections stained with hematoxylin and eosin but were augmented by special stains and transmission electron microscopy. It is anticipated that emerging techniques of molecular biology will help clarify the biological relevance of the histologic types (Gillett et al. 1992).

The principal source of material for this chapter came from studies of young beagle dogs given inhalation exposures to ^{239}PuO$_2$ (at PNNL) or beta-emitting radionuclides in insoluble forms (at ITRI) for life-span dose effects observations (Park et al. 1986; McClellan et al. 1986). A unique feature of the studies done at PNNL was that mastectomies were performed on all the female dogs before exposure to prevent metastatic mammary tumors in the lung that could be confused with primary lung tumors. In this project, there were 66 lung tumors observed in 54 dogs (51 exposed dogs and 3 control dogs). For the purposes of recording the results, multiple tumors of the same histologic type found in different lobes were generally considered one primary tumor with intrapulmonary metastases. The classification system (Table 4.1) includes diagnoses made in other studies as well (Hahn et al. 1973; Hahn, Muggenburg, and Griffith 1992).

DESCRIPTIONS

Epidermoid Carcinoma (Squamous Cell Carcinoma)

The architecture is replaced by an irregular proliferation of stratified squamous epithelium, a few to several cells thick (Figure 4.1–4.2). The stratified squamous epithelium frequently lines large cystic cavities partially filled with necrotic debris. These cavities replace alveoli but leave intact the smaller bronchi; an apparent continuum of the stratified squamous epithelium and bronchial mucosa is frequently observed. The surfaces of the stratified squamous epithelium are generally nonkeratinized. Intercellular bridges and occasional keratin whorls are present. Ultrastructurally, tonofilaments and desmosomes are prominent. Invasion of blood vessels occasionally occurs. Metastases sometimes occur to the tracheobronchial lymph nodes and systemic organs.

Table 4.1. Lung Neoplasia Nomenclature, Index of Figures, Snodog Database Codes, and Incidence.

Diagnosis	Figure	SNODOG Morphology Code[a]	Percent Incidence P[b]	U[c]
Epidermoid carcinoma	4.1–2	M807030	5	
Adenorcarcinoma				
Bronchioloalveolar carcinoma	4.3–4	M825030	39	19
Papillary adenocarcinoma	4.5	M826030	32	66
Solid carcinoma	4.6	M823030	1	0
Adenosquamous carcinoma	4.7	M856030	23	9
Anaplastic carcinoma		M802030	0	0
Small cell		M800230		
Large cell	4.8	M801230		
Sarcoma			0	
Hemangiosarcoma	4.9	M912030	0	30
Fibrosarcoma	4.10	M881030		
Chondrosarcoma	4.11	M922030		
Leiomyosarcoma	4.12	M889030		
Malignant fibrous histiocytoma	4.13	M883030		
Osteosarcoma	4.14	M918030		
Mixed tumor, malignant	4.15	M894030	0	0
Carcinoid tumor, malignant	4.16	M824030	0	0
Benign lung tumors			0	
Adenoma	4.17	M814000	0	0
Papillary adenoma	4.18	M826000		
Fibroma	4.19	M881000		
Carcinoid tumor, benign		M824000		
Mixed tumor, benign	4.20	M808140		
Bronchial gland			0	3
Adenoma	4.21	M81400B		
Adenocarcinoma		M81403B		
Mesothelioma			0	
Benign		M905000	0	0
Malignant	4.22	M905030		
Non-neoplastic lesions				
Adenomatous hyperplasia		M724901		
Squamous metaplasia		M724903		
Radiation pneumonitis	4.23	M497701		

[a] SNOMED code with shaded 6th character added for beagle specific diagnoses.
[b] P = exposed to plutonium dioxide in lifespan studies at PNNL.
[c] U = unexposed longevity study controls (17) and breeding colony dogs (15) at ITRI.

Adenocarcinoma

Bronchioloalveolar Carcinoma

Bronchioloalveolar carcinomas consist of a proliferation of cuboidal to low-columnar, nonciliated epithelium along alveolar septa (Figure 4.3). The cells tend to pile up on the surface and may slough into the lumen of alveoli. In larger masses there is some tendency toward papillary proliferation. The epithelial cells have round to oval, nuclei, with evenly distributed chromatin and indistinct nucleoli. The cytoplasm is homogenous, negative for mucus stains, and may have tapered apical cytoplasm. The stroma is scant but has a tendency for foci of osseous metaplastia (Figure 4.4). There is a tendency for fronds of epithelial cells to extend into adjacent alveoli. Lymphatic invasion may be very prominent in larger masses. Invasion of blood vessels and nerves is unusual. Multiple masses are often present in several lobes. For purposes of coding, the lobe with the largest mass is considered the primary site, and smaller masses are considered metastatic sites.

Papillary Adenocarcinoma

The predominant feature is the papillary proliferation of nonciliated columnar epithelial cells on a fibrovascular stroma that may be fine or coarse (Figure 4.5). The neoplastic cells compress or replace normal architecture of the lung. The lining epithelial cells are usually columnar but may be cuboidal, and form a single layer of cells with basilar nuclei. The individual nuclei may have clumped chromatic and prominent nucleoli. The epithelial cells seldom stain for mucus but there is frequently mucus-positive material in the lumen. The stroma frequently has prominent spicules of metaplastic bone. Lymphatic invasion and metastases are frequent, as with bronchioloalveolar carcinomas.

Solid Carcinoma

The general appearance is solid sheets and chords of anaplastic epithelial cells replacing normal architecture of the lung (Figure 4.6). The individual cells generally have scant cytoplasm and large nuclei with prominent nucleoli.

Adenosquamous Carcinoma (Combined Carcinoma)

These tumors contain mixtures of morphologic patterns of adenocarcinomas and epidermoid carcinomas (Figure 4.7). The papillary pattern is the usual morphologic form of adenocarcinoma present. Prominent portions of both patterns need to be present, at least one fourth of one morphologic pattern or the other. The glandular proliferation tends to form tubules or ducts with prominent stroma and to form a continuum with nonstratified squamous epithelium.

Anaplastic Carcinoma

Small-Cell Carcinoma

None of these tumors has been reported in the beagle colonies at ANL; University of California, Davis; ITRI; PNNL; or University of Utah.

Large-Cell Carcinoma

The tumor is characterized by large anaplastic epithelial cells that have abundant eosinophilic cytoplasm and large nuclei, with prominent large nucleoli (Figure 4.8). Multiple nuclei may be present. The individual cells or clumps of cells fill the alveoli but do not invade large interstitial structures of the lung. The anaplastic cells appear to arise from alveolar epithelial lining cells.

Lung

Sarcoma

Hemangiosarcoma

These sarcomas of vascular endothelial origin arise from the alveolar regions and have cavernous or capillary patterns (Figure 4.9). They consist of blood-filled cavities lined with plump anaplastic endothelial cells, having large oval nuclei with prominent nucleoli. The cytoplasm is flattened and homogenous. Hemorrhage frequently extends into alveoli and tissues surrounding the neoplasms. Widespread metastases frequently occur.

Fibrosarcoma

These tumors consist of spindle-shaped cells with anaplastic nuclei and resemble fibrosarcomas in other organs of the body (Figure 4.10). In the lungs of irradiated dogs these tumors originate in alveolar portions of the lungs. Metastases may occur.

Chondrosarcoma

The tumor consists of confluent lobules of hyaline cartilage (Figure 4.11). The lobules, which are not supplied with blood vessels, have degeneration in the center. The lobules appear to be expanding with an increased density of mildly anaplastic chondrocytes toward the periphery of the lobules.

Leiomyosarcoma

The tumor consists of an irregular proliferation of anaplastic smooth-muscle cells originating in bronchial walls (Figure 4.12).

Malignant Fibrous Histiocytoma

This is a solitary tumor that arises in the hilar region and may invade airways and arteries (Figure 4.13). Metastasis, however, is to local lymph nodes. The tumor is composed of a mixture of histiocytes and fibroblasts. The fibrous tissue has a swirled and, occasionally, a storiform pattern. The histiocytic cells may be very pleomorphic, and giant, multinucleated cells may be present. In only one case has this tumor been found as a primary lung tumor.

Osteosarcoma

In the lungs of irradiated dogs, these tumors are composed of hyperchromatic pyriform cells (osteoblasts) that produce varying amounts of connective tissue and immature bone. Frequently, mineralized bone spicules are present. In these histologic features, the osteosarcomas of the lung resemble such tumors elsewhere in the body. Most of these osteosarcomas appear to arise from osseous metaplasia in the stroma of lung carcinomas (Figure 4.14).

Mixed Tumor, Malignant

These are large confluent masses of proliferating fibroblasts mixed with ducts or glands of anaplastic epithelial cells (Figure 4.15).

Carcinoid Tumors

These tumors are rare in the dog and have not been reported in the beagle dog colonies at ANL; University of California, Davis; PNNL; or University of Utah. An atypical neuroendocrine carcinoma has been reported (Harkema et al. 1992) in an unexposed dog in the ITRI (Figure 4.16). This tumor was a nonencapsulated solid carcinoma composed of lobules of closely packed, round-to-oval cells separated by a fine stroma. The cells had abundant eosinophilic or clear cytoplasm that contained dense core granules and had neuron-specific enolase staining.

Benign Lung Tumors

Adenoma

A focal proliferation of cuboidal epithelial cells that conform to an alveolar (Figure 4.17) or papillary (Figure 4.18) pattern. The individual cells are uniform and regular and form a single lining layer. The cell nuclei are uniform, without prominent nucleoli. The surrounding alveolar parenchyma is compressed.

Fibroma

A focal proliferation of fibroblasts producing abundant fibrous tissue (Figure 4.19). They usually occur in the parenchyma of the lung.

Carcinoid Tumor, Benign

None of these tumors has been reported in the beagle colonies at ANL; University of California, Davis; ITRI; PNNL; or University of Utah.

Mixed Tumor, Benign

A glandular and fibrous proliferation not infiltrating adjacent pulmonary parenchyma (Figure 4.20).

Bronchial Gland Tumors

Adenoma

A focal proliferation of mucus-producing cells supported by a thick, fibrous stroma. These tumors are associated with the larger airways.

Adenocarcinoma

An infrequent tumor that has a close association with bronchi. These tumors form glandular structures lined by a high-columnar epithelium (Figure 4.21).

Mesothelioma

Mesotheliomas arise from the mesothelium without apparent involvement of pulmonary parenchyma. They consist of a papillary proliferation of anaplastic cells without associated fibrous stromas (Figure 4.22).

Adenomatous Hyperplasia

Adenomatous hyperplasia consists of the focal proliferation of alveolar or bronchiolar epithelial cells that line alveolar septa with cuboidal or low-columnar epithelium. The alveolar architecture is retained, and the epithelial proliferation is not clearly associated with inflammatory reactions. This contrasts with the more diffuse, reactive, alveolar epithelial hyperplasia associated with radiation pneumonitis and with bronchioloalveolar neoplasms, where the normal architecture of the lung is replaced.

Squamous Metaplasia

Squamous metaplasia can occur in alveolar regions of the lung without any clear association with bronchioles or bronchi. It is frequently associated with pulmonary fibrosis.

Radiation Pneumonitis

Acute radiation pneumonitis due to inhalation of radionuclides is characterized by congestion, alveolar inflammatory exudates, interstitial cellular infiltrates, desquamation of bronchiolar and

Lung

alveolar epithelium with epithelial regression, vascular injury and repair, and pulmonary fibrosis (Slauson et al. 1976, Slauson, Hahn, and Chiffelle 1977). Conspicuous vascular and interstitial inflammatory reactions are much more prominent in animals exposed to beta-emitting radionuclides.

Chronic radiation pneumonitis due to the inhalation of radionuclides is characterized by interstitial fibrosis associated with alveolar epithelial cell hyperplasia and increased numbers of alveolar macrophages (Figure 4.23). Interstitial cellular infiltrates and vascular obliterative lesions may also be present. The interstitial fibrosis has a multifocal distribution primarily associated with subpleural and peribronchial areas of all lobes. Autoradiographs show alpha-emitting radionuclides concentrated in the areas of interstitial fibrosis.

REFERENCES

Gillett, N. A., B. L. Stegelmeier, G. Kelly, P. J. Haley, and F. F. Hahn. 1992. Expression of epidermal growth factor receptor in plutonium-239-induced lung neoplasms in dogs. *Vet. Pathol* 29:46-52.

Hahn, F. F., S. A. Benjamin, B. B. Boecker, T. L. Chiffelle, C. H. Hobbs, R. K. Jones, R. O. McClellan, J. A. Pickrell, and R. C. Redman. 1973. Primary pulmonary neoplasms in beagle dogs exposed to aerosols to ^{144}Ce in fused-clay particles. *J. Natl. Cancer Inst.* 50:675-698.

Hahn, F. F., B. A. Muggenburg, and W. C. Griffith. 1993. Primary Lung Cancer in the Longevity Study/Control Population of the ITRI Beagle Dog Colony, pp. 133-136. In: *Inhalation Toxicology Research Institute Annual Report 1991-1992*, G. L. Finch, K. J. Nikula, and P. L. Bradley, Eds. LMF-138, NTIS, Springfield, VA.

Harkema, J. R., S. E. Jones, D. K. Naydan, and D. W. Wilson. 1992. An atypical neuroendocrine tumor in the lung of a beagle dog. *Vet. Pathol.* 29:175-179.

McClellan, R. O., B. B. Boecker, F. F. Hahn, and B. A. Muggenburg. 1986. Lovelace ITRI Studies on the Toxicity of Inhaled Radionuclides in Beagle Dogs, pp. 74-96. In: *Life-Span Radiation Effects Studies in Animals: What Can They Tell Us?*, R. C. Thompson and J. A. Mahaffey, Eds. CONF-830951, NTIS, Springfield, VA.

Moulton, J. E. 1978. Tumors of the Respiratory System, pp. 205-239. In: *Tumors in Domestic Animals*, J. E. Moulton, Ed. University of California Press, Berkeley, CA.

Moulton, J. E., C. von Tscharner, and R. Schneider. 1981. Classification of lung carcinomas in the dog and cat. *Vet. Pathol.* 18:513-528.

Park, J. F., G. E. Dagle, H. A. Ragan, R. E. Weller, and D. L. Stevens. 1986. Current Status of Life-Span Studies with Inhaled Plutonium in Beagles at Pacific Northwest Laboratory, pp. 455-470. In: *Life-Span Radiation Effects Studies in Animals: What Can They Tell Us?*, R. C. Thompson and J. A. Mahaffey, eds. CONF-830951, NTIS, Springfield, VA.

Slauson, D.O., F.F. Hahn, S.A. Benjamin, T.L. Chiffelle, and R.K. Jones. 1976. Inflammatory sequences in acute pulmonary radiation injury. *Am. J. Pathol.* 82:549-572.

Slauson, D.O., F.F. Hahn, and T.L. Chiffelle. 1977. The pulmonary vascular pathology of experimental radiation pneumonitis. *Am. J. Pathol.* 88:635-654.

World Health Organization. *International Histologic Classification of Tumours in Domestic Animals*, Bulletin WHO 50:1-144 (1974) and 50:145-282 (1976) WHO, Geneva, Switzerland.

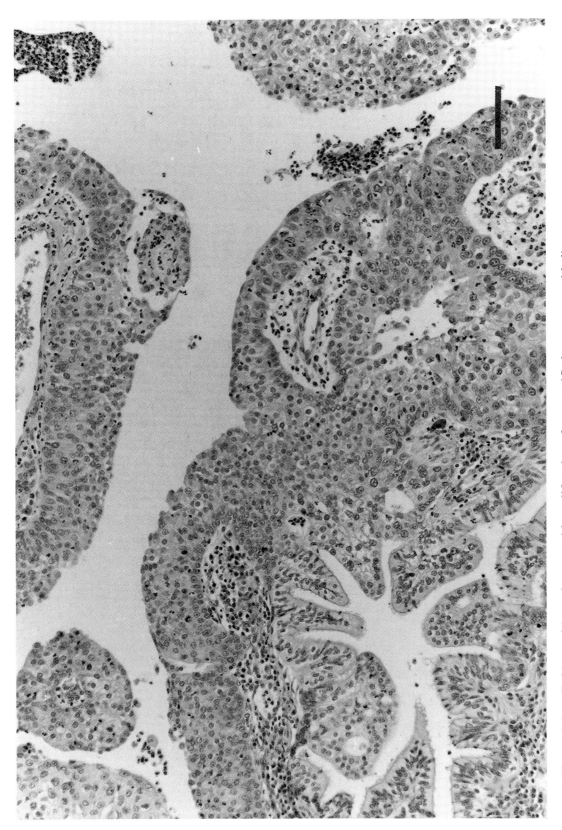

Figure 4.1. Epidermoid carcinoma, with proliferation of nonstratified squamous epithelium *(dog 796). H&E. Bar = 80 µm.*

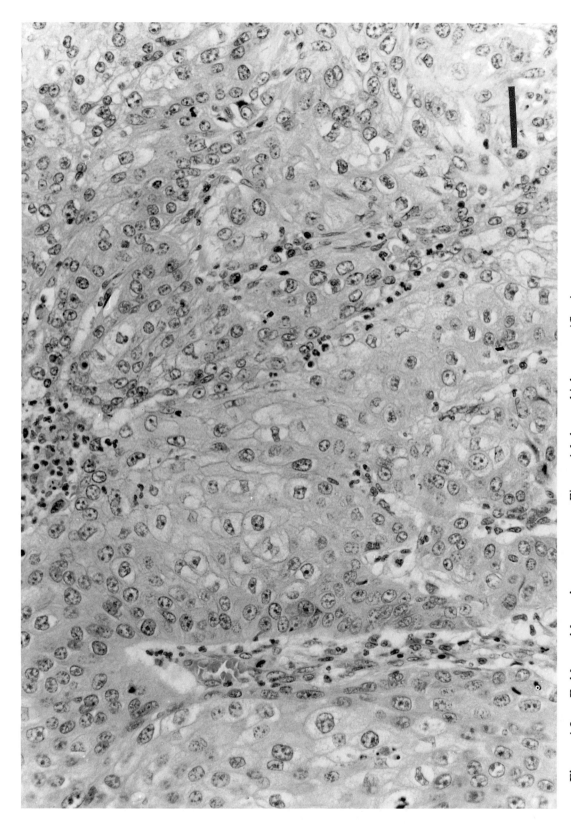

Figure 4.2. Epidermoid carcinoma, same as Figure 4.1, but at higher magnification. *H&E. Bar = 40 μm.*

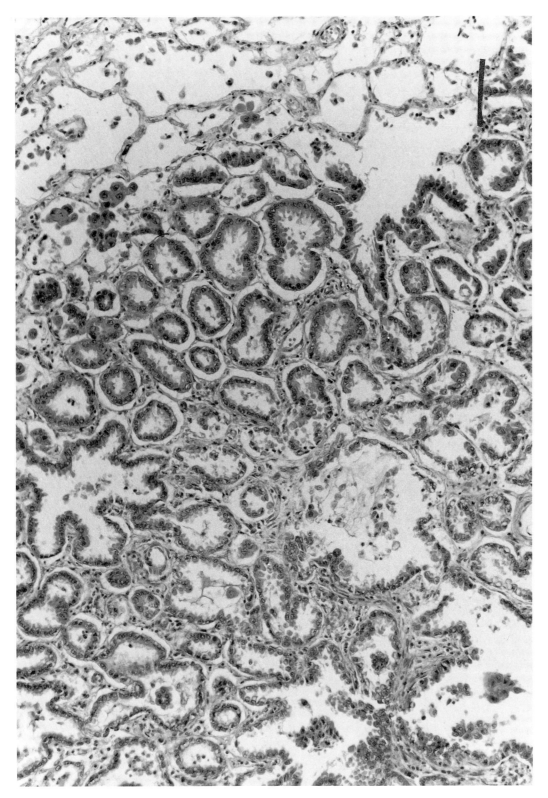

Figure 4.3. **Bronchioloalveolar carcinoma**, alveolar pattern of proliferating cuboidal epithelial cells *(dog 1631). H&E.*
Bar = 80 µm.

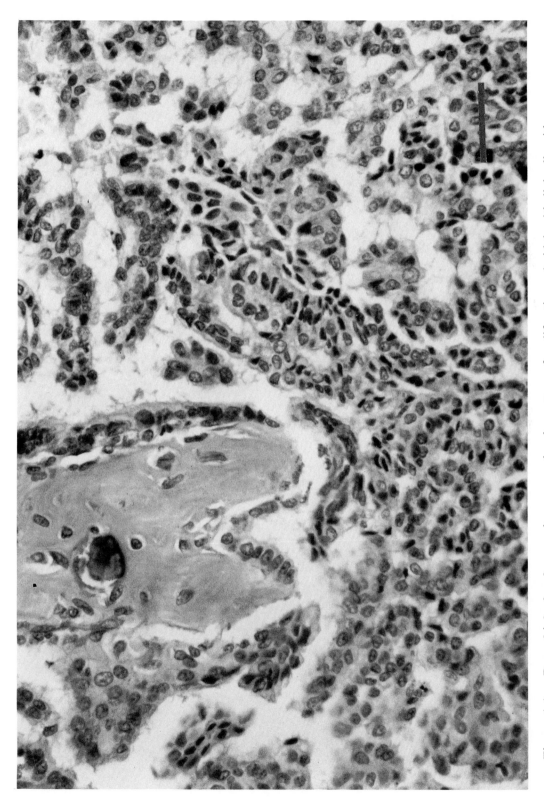

Figure 4.4. **Bronchioloalveolar carcinoma**, an alveolar pattern of proliferating cuboidal epithelial cells with osseous metaplasia. *H&E. Bar = 40 μm.*

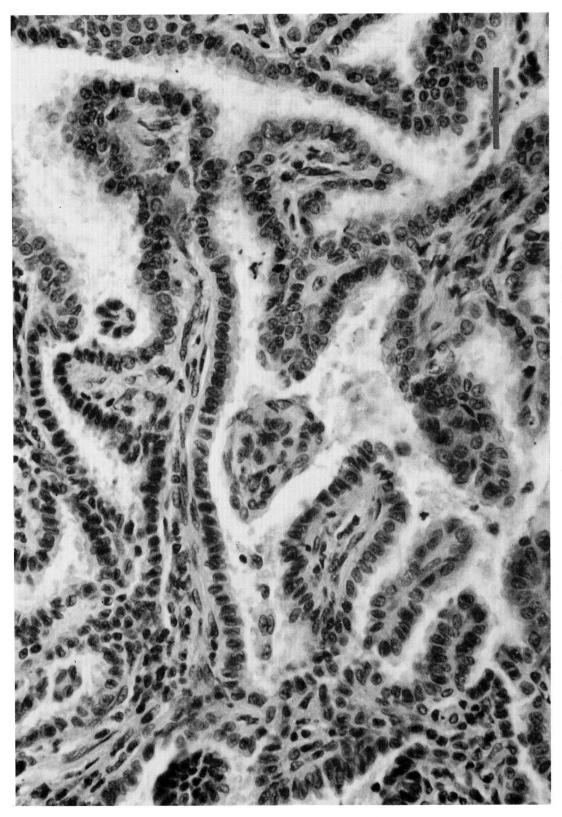

Figure 4.5. Papillary adenocarcinoma, a papillary pattern of low-columnar epithelial cells *(dog 757). H&E. Bar = 40 μm.*

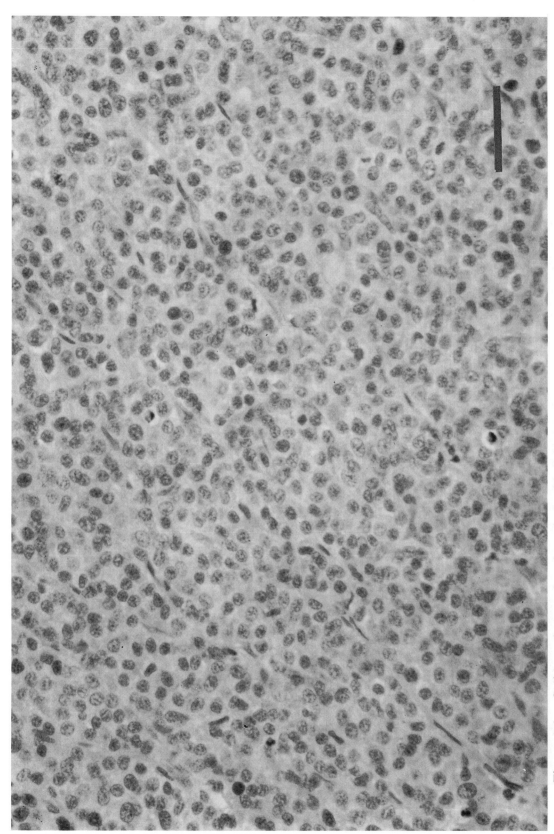

Figure 4.6. Solid carcinoma, densely packed epithelial cells with a very fine stroma *(dog 805). H&E. Bar = 40 μm.*

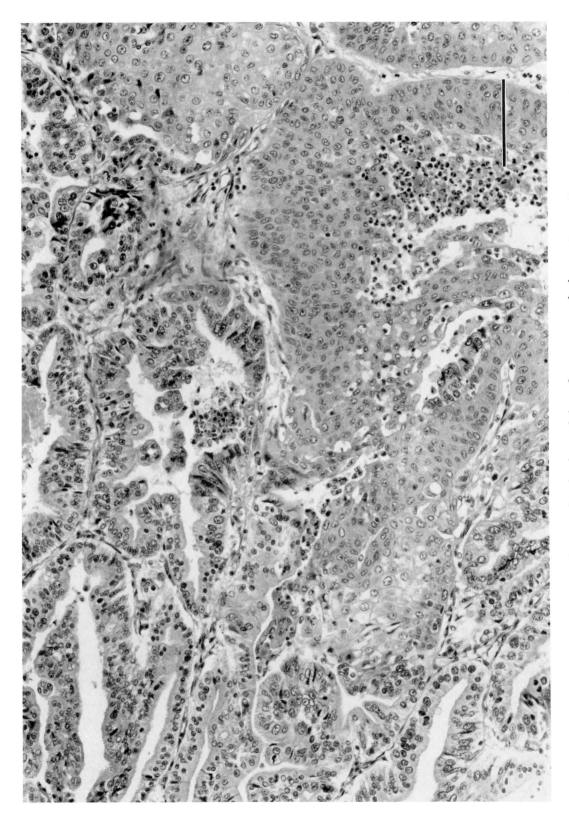

Figure 4.7.   Adenosquamous carcinoma, showing intermixing of squamous and adenomatous patterns. *H&E. Bar = 80 μm.*

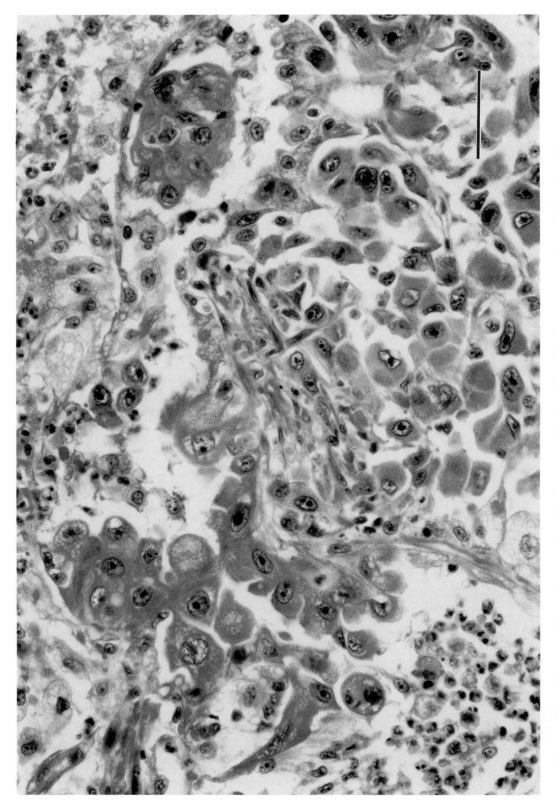

Figure 4.8. Large-cell carcinoma, showing large anaplastic cells with abundant cytoplasm filling alveoli. *H&E. Bar = 40 μm.*

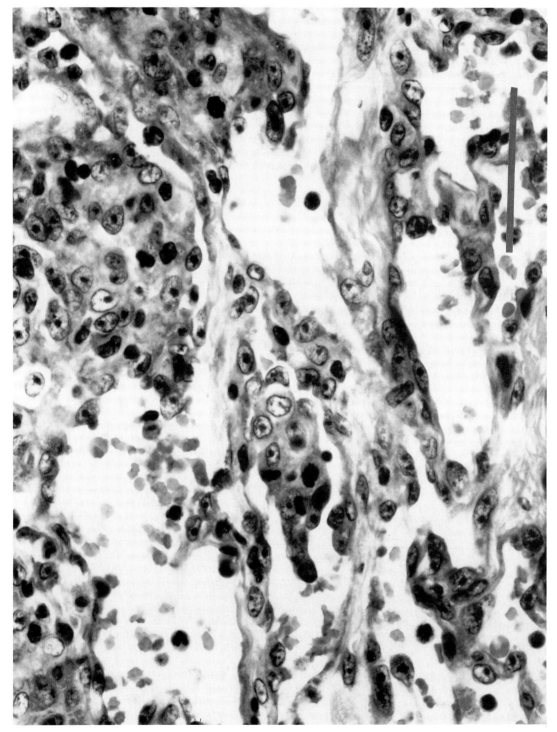

Figure 4.9. Hemangiosarcoma, showing the plump nuclei of anaplastic cells lining vascular space. *H&E. Bar = 45 µm.*

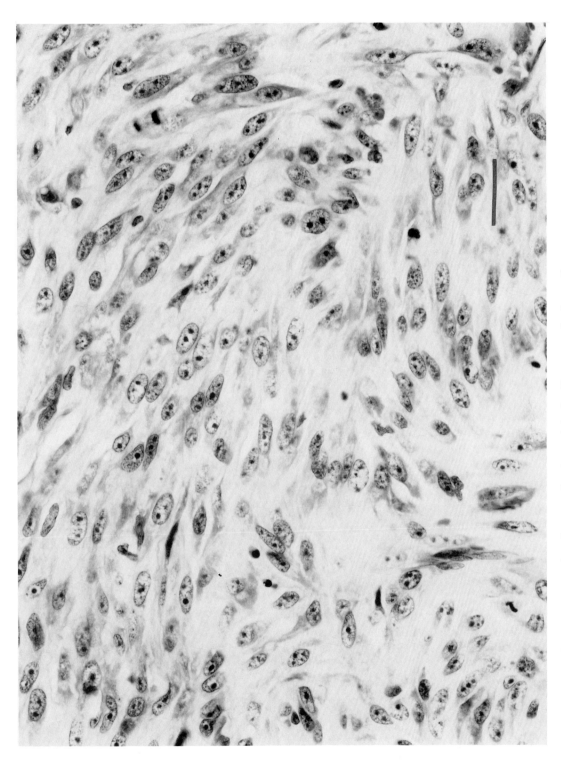

Figure 4.10. Fibrosarcoma, showing anaplastic nuclei of collagen-producing cells. *H&E. Bar = 16 μm.*

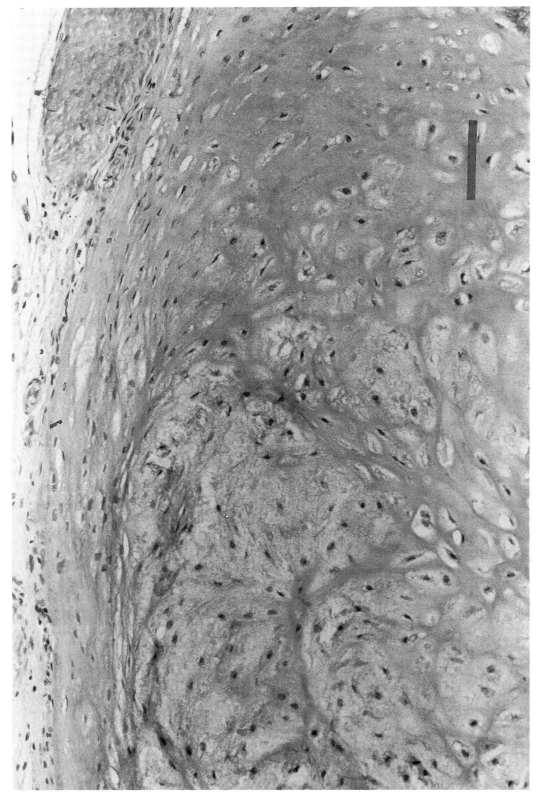

Figure 4.11. **Chondrosarcoma**; expanding avascular cartilaginous tissue with degeneration and necrosis in the center *(dog 1772). H&E. Bar = 80 µm.*

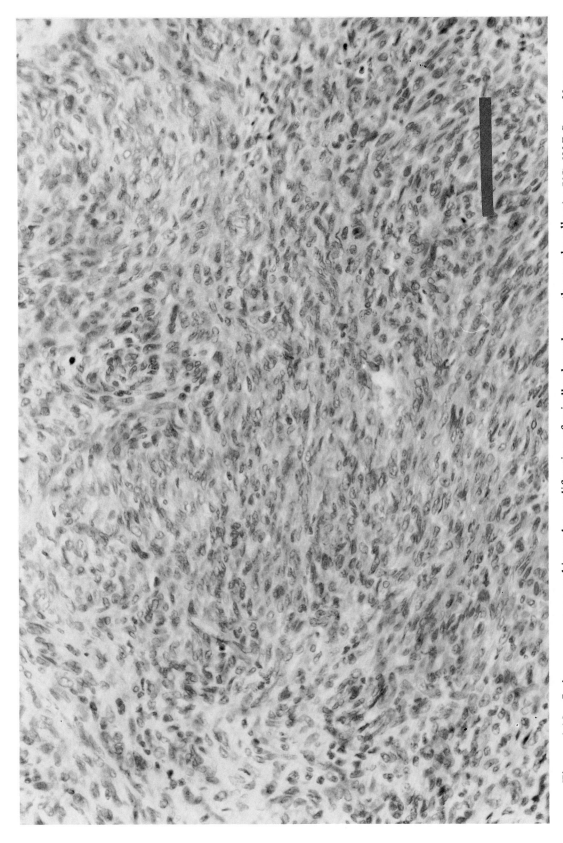

Figure 4.12. Leiomyosarcoma and irregular proliferation of spindle-shaped, smooth-muscle cells *(dog 797). H&E. Bar = 80 µm.*

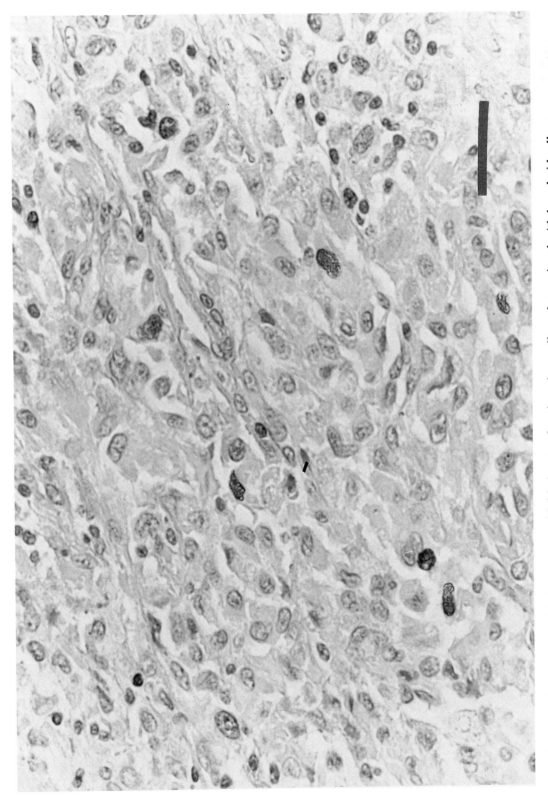

Figure 4.13. Malignant **histiocytoma**, with histiocytes forming giant cells and associated with lymphoid cells *(dog 1513). H&E. Bar = 40 μm.*

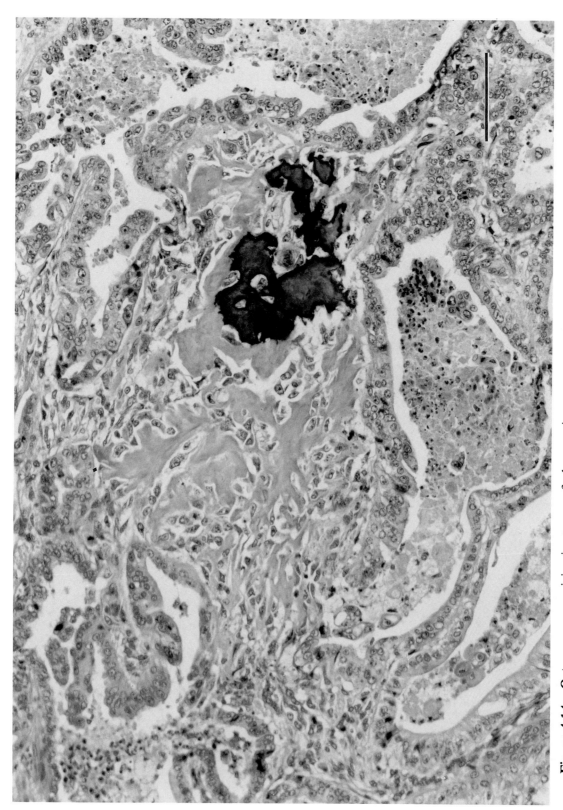

Figure 4.14. Osteosarcoma arising in storma of adenocarcinoma. *H&E. Bar = 80 μm.*

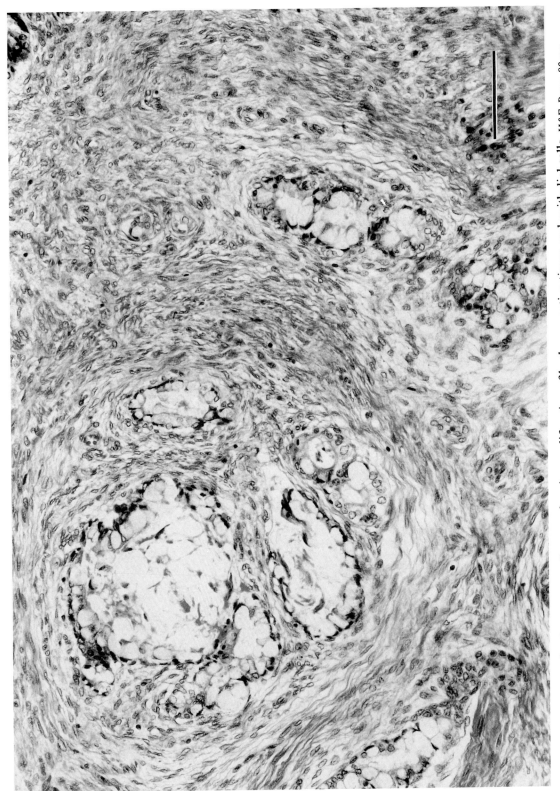

Figure 4.15. Mixed tumors, malignant, showing proliferation of both connective tissue and epithelial cells. *H&E. Bar = 80 μm.*

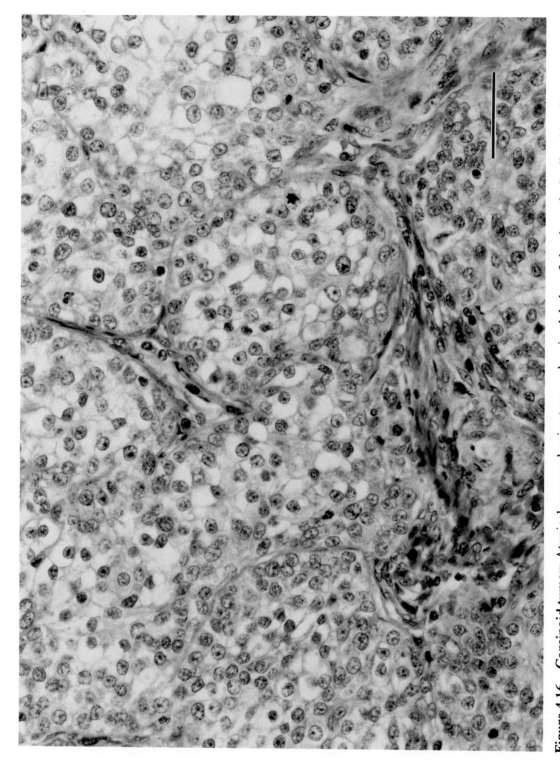

Figure 4.16. **Carcinoid tumor:** *Atypical neuroendocrine tumor, showing lobules of closely packed cells with a fine stroma.* *H&E. Bar = 40 μm.*

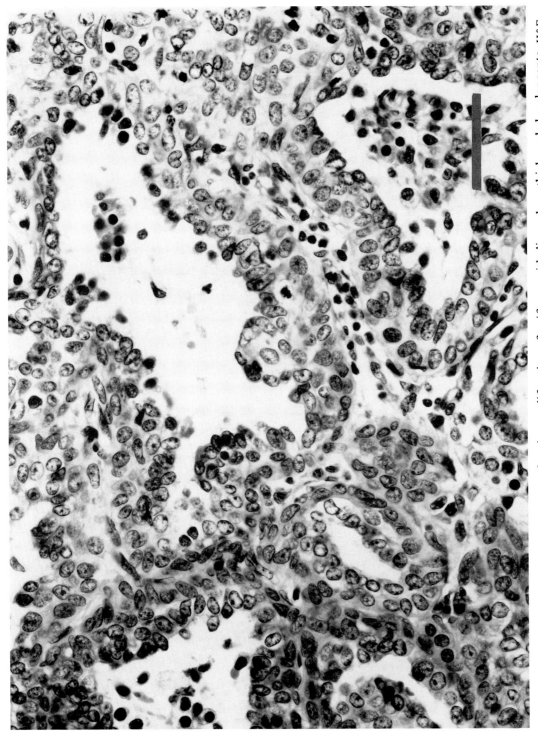

Figure 4.17. Adenoma, alveolar pattern; showing proliferation of uniform epithelium along thickened alveolar septa. *H&E. Bar = 40 μm.*

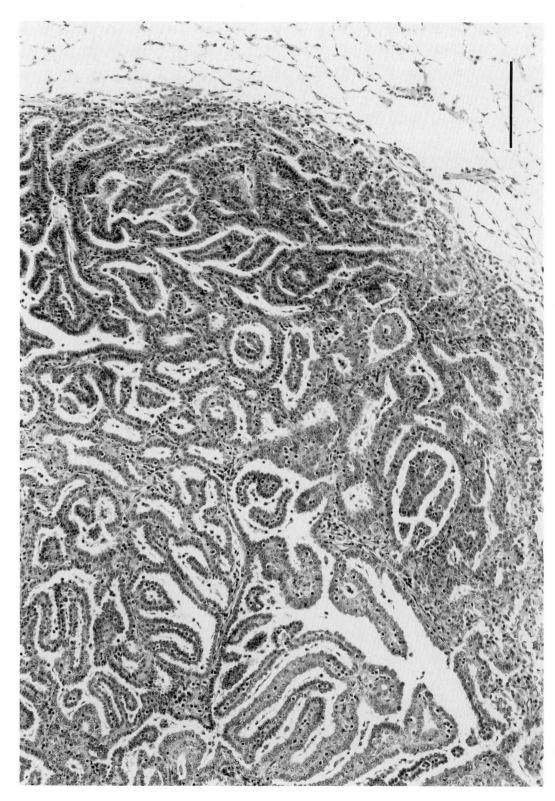

Figure 4.18. **Adenoma, papillary** form; showing proliferation of uniform epithelial cells in a papillary pattern. *H&E.*
Bar = 120 μm.

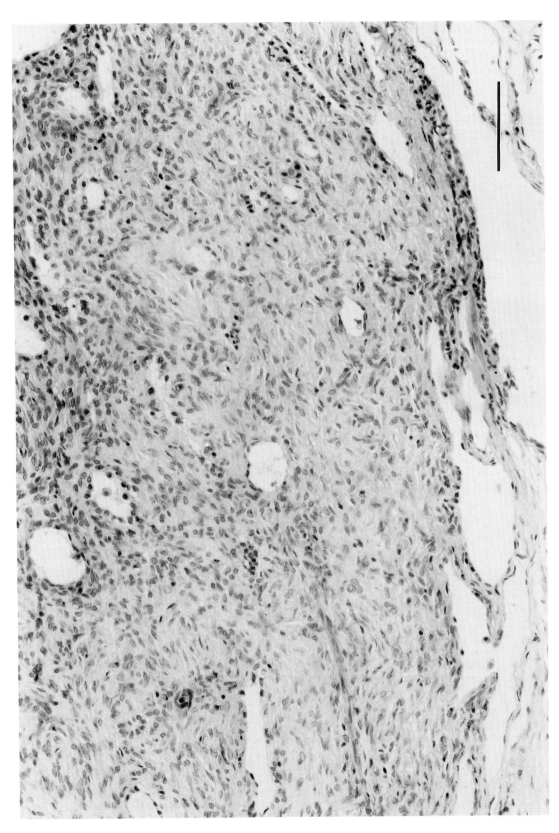

Figure 4.19. Fibroma, showing proliferation of fibroblasts with entrapment of alveolar structures. *H&E. Bar = 80 μm.*

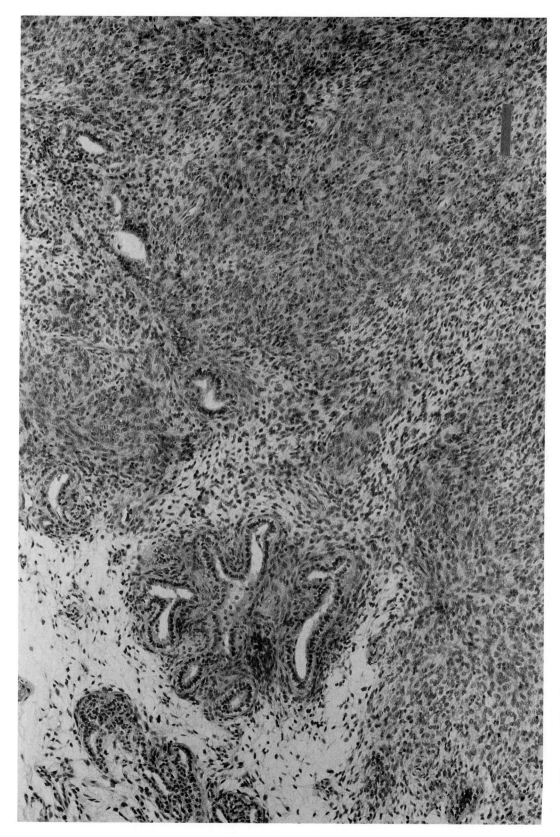

Figure 4.20. Benign mixed tumor; proliferation of both glandular and connective-tissue cells *(dog 1419). H&E. Bar = 80 µm.*

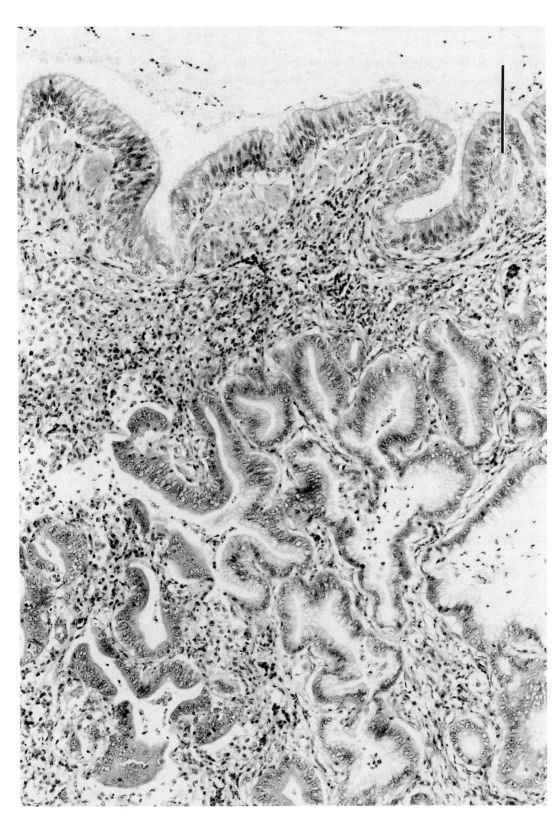

Figure 4.21. Bronchial gland adenocarcinoma, showing glandular structures adjacent to airway. *H&E. Bar = 120 µm.*

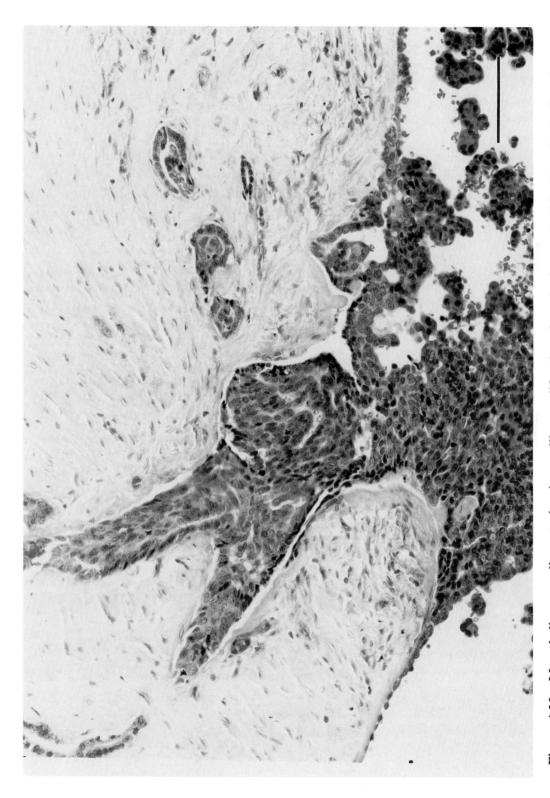

Figure 4.22. **Mesothelioma, malignant,** showing papillary proliferation of anaplastic mesothelial cells and induction of fibrosis *(dog 1222), H&E. Bar = 80 μm.*

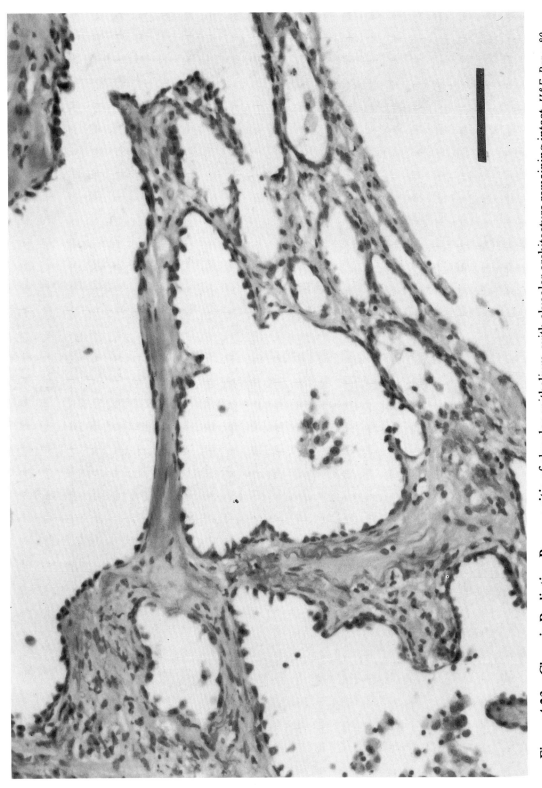

Figure 4.23. Chronic Radiation Pneumonitis of alveolar epithelium, with alveolar architecture remaining intact. *H&E. Bar = 80 μm.*

CHAPTER 5: Thyroid Tumors

Patrick J. Haley
Inhalation Toxicology Research Institute
(Currently at Nycomed Inc.)

Stephen A. Benjamin
Colorado State University

INTRODUCTION

Because beagles have been reported to be at increased risk over other breeds of dogs for the development of spontaneous thyroid neoplasms, it is important to establish the histological characteristics of thyroid tumors in control populations of this breed. The beagle colonies at the Department Of Energy/Office of Health and Environmental Research contract laboratories afford a unique opportunity to study spontaneous thyroid neoplasms in populations of normal dogs with lifetime health histories and to determine the effect of various carcinogens on the thyroid gland. This chapter should be considered an extenstion of earlier work reported by: Brodey and Kelley 1968, Van Sandersleben and Hanichem 1974, Hayes and Fraumeni 1975, Leav et al. 1976, Mitchell, Hurov and Troy 1979, Birchard and Roesel 1981, and Harari, Patterson, and Rosenthal 1986.

An outline of principal lesions observed in beagle dogs, with an index to illustrations and SNOMED database codes, is shown in Table 5.1.

DESCRIPTIONS

Follicular Hyperplasia

Nodular hyperplasia is a frequently encountered incidental lesion of old dogs. These lesions are usually nonfunctional. Nodular hyperplasia is characterized by multiple irregular foci of hyperplastic follicular cells that are sharply delineated but not encapsulated from adjacent tissue. Histologic characteristics are variable and include small follicles containing little or no colloid, or hyperplastic columnar cells lining large, dilated, cystic spaces with abundant, deeply staining colloid present (Figure 5.1). Compression of adjacent thyroid parenchyma is not usually observed.

Idiopathic Follicular Atrophy

In idiopathic follicular atrophy, progressive loss of degenerating follicular epithelium is accompanied by interstitial infiltration by adipose cells, resulting in the isolation of small aggregates of active follicles. The appearance of increased interstitial connective tissue is more a product of stromal collapse and condensation than fibrosis. Persisting follicular epithelial cells may be hyperplastic, with tall columnar cells lining small follicles filled with deeply eosinophilic and/or vacuolated colloid (Figure 5.2). A small encapsulated adenoma or nonencapsulated area of nodular hyperplasia may be present also in affected glands. Inflammatory cells (lymphocytes and/or macrophages) are not usually present.

Table 5.1. Thyroid Neoplasia nomenclature, index to figures, and SNODOG database codes

Nomenclature	Figure(s)	SNODOG Morphology code[a]
Non-neoplastic		
Follicular hyperplasia	5.1	M72000F
Idiopathic follicular atrophy	5.2	M580005
Lymphocytic thyroiditis	5.3	M430000
Benign Tumors		
Follicular adenoma	5.4	M833000
Other non-neoplastic lesions	5.5–8	
Malignant		
Follicular carcinoma	5.9	M833030
Solid carcinoma	5.10–12	M823030
Solid follicular carcinoma	5.13–17	M823033
Oxyphil tumor	5.18–19	M829030
Papillary carcinoma		M805030
Squamous cell carcinoma		M807030
Anaplastic carcinoma		M802030
C-cell carcinoma		M851030
Ectopic thyroid tumor		[b] T
Other neoplastic lesions		

[a] SNOMED code with shaded 6th character added for beagle specific diagnoses.
[b] Use appropriate SNOMED code with "T" as 6th character.

Lymphocytic Thyroiditis

Spontaneous lymphocytic thyroiditis is an autoimmune disease with a genetic basis that occurs frequently in some beagle colonies. Lymphocytic thyroiditis is characterized by multifocal to diffuse infiltration of the thyroid by lymphocytes, plasma cells, and macrophages that penetrate between follicle-lining cells and accumulate with follicular lumens, along with degenerative epithelial cells. Nodular lymphoid accumulation with the thyroid may be observed, accompanied by follicular degeneration and interstitial fibrosis (Figure 5.3). Concomitant C-cell hyperplasia may be noted.

Follicular Adenoma

Grossly, follicular adenomas appear as small, well-demarcated, solid, tan-to-dark brown nodules. Follicular tumors are considered benign upon histologic examination when they are encapsulated by a fibrous connective tissue capsule, compress surrounding tissue, and display uniform cellular characteristics (Figure 5.4). The capsule may be thick and surround the nodule entirely, or thin and incomplete but without extension of the mass into adjacent tissue. Variably thick, fibrous connective tissue bands may arise from the capsule and penetrate irregularly into the mass. Follicular tumors are typically microfollicular with some areas of solid cord development. They may be singular or multiple, making differentiation from nodular hyperplasia difficult. Neoplastic cells have uniformly rounded and slightly vesiculate nuclei with single nucleoli. Cells are cuboidal to polygonal and contain ample granular eosinophilic to basophilic cytoplasm. In some areas, the cytoplasm may be

markedly vacuolated. The cells may be arranged in small aggregates or narrow twisting cords, two to four cells thick, surrounded by a thin fibrovascular stroma. Mitotic figures are not usually apparent.

Other Non-Neoplastic Lesions

There is as yet no prognostic significance for subdivisions of benign tumors such as papillary, cystic, solid, or combinations thereof. Tumors with a solid follicular pattern are usually grouped under the broader title of follicular adenomas (Figures 5.5 and 5.6). Cystic adenomas are well-delineated, tan-to-dark brown nodules, with a cystic center filled with serosanguinous fluid (Figures 5.7 and 5.8). The wall of the cyst may be fibrous and lined with single to multiple layers of cuboidal to tall columnar epithelial cells and variably sized, arborizing papillary fronds projecting into the cyst lumen. Solid papillary adenomas are characterized by cuboidal to columnar epithelial cells resting on linear and branching papillary fronds without definite cyst formation.

Follicular Carcinoma

Follicular carcinomas are characterized by a predominance of follicular differentiation with cells forming both macrofollicular and microfollicular patterns that are accompanied occasionally by tubular and papilliferous areas (Figure 5.9). The size of follicles may be constant or may vary considerably throughout the tumor, with larger follicles becoming irregular and linear in some areas. Follicular lining cells may be cuboidal to tall columnar with basally located, vesicular nuclei and ample eosinophilic cytoplasm. Staining may be more basophilic in those tumors with decreased amounts of cytoplasm. Production of colloid is variable and, typically, most intense within larger follicles; small follicles and acinar structures may be devoid of colloid. While capsular and vascular invasion occurs often, cellular pleomorphism and atypia do not. Stromal development is variable.

Solid Carcinoma

Solid thyroid carcinomas are characterized by large numbers of neoplastic epithelial cells arranged in densely cellular sheets, thick multicellular cords, and/or small to large irregularly shaped aggregates separated by a variably thick fibrovascular stroma (Figures 5.10, 5.11, and 5.12). Cords of cells, which vary from 2 to 20 or more cells thick, may occur in linear twisting patterns that occasionally suggest tubular and papillary structures. The fibrovascular stroma may progress from very thin strands that separate small aggregates of epithelial cells into micronodules, to thick bands coursing irregularly throughout the mass, breaking it up into larger discrete nodules. In some tumors, the stroma may be quite delicate and barely discernible against the background of solid sheets of neoplastic cells. Severe, centrally located necrosis and hemorrhage are frequently present in some tumors.

The neoplastic epithelial cells are typically large, cuboidal to polygonal, with round to ovoid and vesicular nuclei and singular nucleoli. Cytoplasm is ample, eosinophilic, and granular in most cases; however, some tumors may have cells with a small amount of granular and basophilic to gray cytoplasm. Cellular pleomorphism is not typically prominent but may occur in highly malignant variants, along with increased numbers of mitotic figures. Aggregates of oxyphilic cells may be present and trapped within the background of neoplastic cells.

Capsular invasion and/or vascular penetration are usual in these tumors and form the basis for a diagnosis of malignancy.

Solid Follicular Carcinoma

Solid follicular carcinomas display characteristics previously described for both follicular carcinomas and solid carcinomas, with both components being present in approximately equal ratios (Figures 5.13 through 5.17). The follicular component may be of either the micro- or macrofollicular

pattern and scattered throughout the tumor, or it may alternate with entirely solid regions. As noted previously, nuclear and cellular pleomorphism is infrequent, while capsular and vascular invasion often occurs.

Oxyphil Tumor

A variant of the solid carcinoma is the oxyphil tumor, which is characterized by a somewhat uniform population of polygonal, strongly eosinophilic cells arranged in solid sheets without follicular development (Figures 5.18 and 5.19). Nuclei are slightly pleomorphic, vesiculate, irregularly rounded, and usually located eccentrically within homogenous eosinophilic cytoplasm. While there is extensive penetration by a fine fibrovascular stroma, the neoplastic cells show no specific orientation and may tend to pile up in some areas. Penetration of the capsule and/or vasculature attests to the malignancy of this tumor.

Papillary Carcinoma

Papillary carcinomas, while reported frequently in humans, are rare in dogs and have not been observed in the dogs examined here. Arborizing fibrovascular stalks and papillary fronds predominate, accompanied by a marked follicular pattern.

Squamous Cell Carcinoma

Squamous cell carcinomas of the thyroid have been described in dogs but have not been identified in the beagles considered here. Histologic criteria are the same for squamous cell carcinomas, arising from any other epithelial surface and include keratinizing cells with intercellular bridges. Squamous cell carcinomas arising in the tonsil and metastasizing to the thyroid have been observed. The possibility of such a phenomenon should be carefully evaluated whenever a squamous cell carcinoma is observed in the thyroid.

Anaplastic Carcinoma

Anaplastic or undifferentiated carcinomas of the thyroid have been described in dogs but have not been identified in the beagles considered here. The tumors are typically solid, with a marked degree of cellular cell formation.

C-Cell Carcinoma

C-cell carcinomas are reported occasionally in the dog but have not been identified in the beagles considered here. These tumors are usually solid, with either large or small polygonal cells that may resemble plasma cells. Alternatively, the cells may be columnar and separated into lobules by a fibrovascular stroma. The cells may be lined up perpendicularly to the basement membrane. A diagnostic aid is the presence of an amyloid-containing stroma; however, its occurrence is not invariable for this tumor. Immunoperoxidase techniques used for staining for the presence of calcitonin are a more reliable indicator of the parafollicular origin of these cells.

Ectopic Thyroid Tumors

Neoplasms arising at the base of the heart in beagles have been diagnosed as ectopic thyroid carcinomas, based on ultrastructural characteristics. Cells of the primary tumor and its metastases are characterized as polyhedral, with lightly eosinophilic, finely granular, and, occasionally, vacuolated cytoplasm with scattered PAS-positive granules. Nuclei are variable in size, round to oval, and centrally located. Mitotic figures are present frequently. Ultrastructural characteristics used to

diagnose tumors of thyroid origin include well-developed cytoplasmic organelles, variable numbers of large intracytoplasmic vacuoles, absence of membrane-bound dense granules, and distinctive tubular or rod-like structures in the cytoplasm.

Other Neoplastic Lesions

Thyroid tumors of mesenchymal origin, which include osteosarcoma, chondrosarcoma, carcinosarcoma, and malignant epithelial-mesenchymal tumor, co-existent type, are extremely rare and have not been observed in these beagle colonies. This does not preclude their appearance, and diagnosis depends on the salient features of differentiation.

REFERENCES

Birchard, S. J., and O. F. Roesel. 1981. Neoplasia of the thyroid gland in the dog: a retrospective study of 16 cases. *J. Am. Anim. Hosp. Assoc.* 17:369-372.

Brodey, R. S. and D. F. Kelley. 1968. Thyroid neoplasms in the dog, a clinicopathologic study of fifty-seven cases. *Cancer* 22: 06-416.

Harari, J., J. S. Patterson, and R. C. Rosenthal. 1986. Clinical and pathologic features of thyroid tumors in 26 dogs. *J. Am. Vet. Med. Assoc.* 10:1160-1163.

Hayes, H. M. and J. F. Fraumeni, Jr. 1975. Canine thyroid neoplasms: epidemiologic features. *J. Natl. Cancer Inst.* 55:931-934.

Leav, I., A. L. Schiller, A. Rijnberk, M. A. Legg, and P. J. Der Kinderen. 1976. Adenomas and carcinomas of the canine and feline thyroid. *Am. J. Pathol.* 83:61-122.

Mitchell M., L. I. Hurov, and G. C. Troy. 1979. Canine thyroid carcinomas: clinical occurrence, staging by means of scintiscans and therapy of 15 cases. *Vet. Surg.* 8:112-118.

Van Sandersleben, J. and T. Hanichem. 1974. Chapter III, Tumors of the Thyroid Gland, pp. 35-42. In: *The Bulletin of the World Health Organization, International Histological Classification of Tumors of Domestic Animals,* World Health Organization, Geneva, Switzerland.

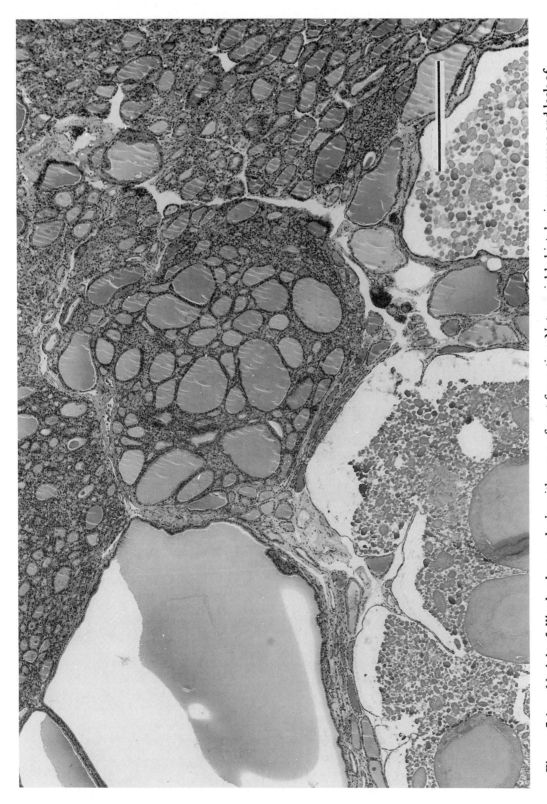

Figure 5.1. Nodular **follicular hyperplasia** with areas of cyst formation. Note variable histologic appearance and lack of capsule. *Bar = 50 μm.*

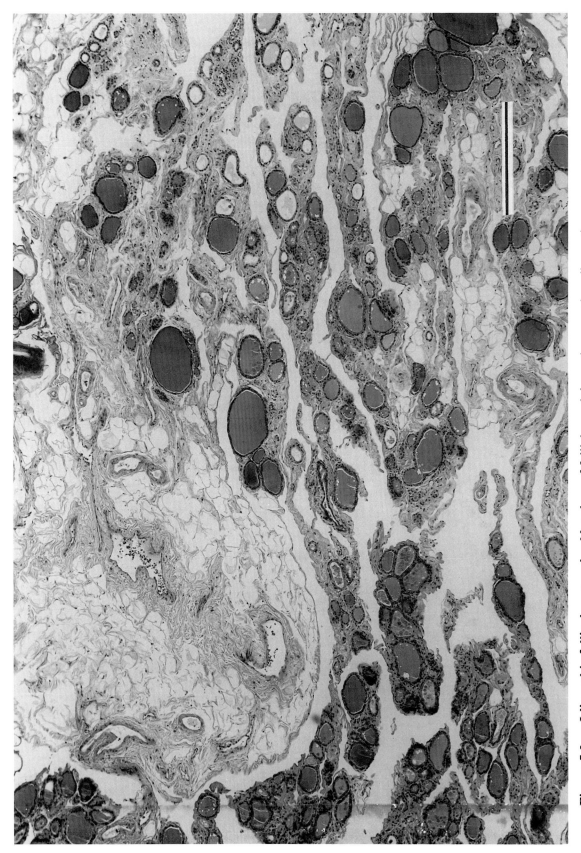

Figure 5.2. **Idiopathic follicular atrophy.** Note loss of follicles and the replacement by adipose tissue. *Bar = 50 μm.*

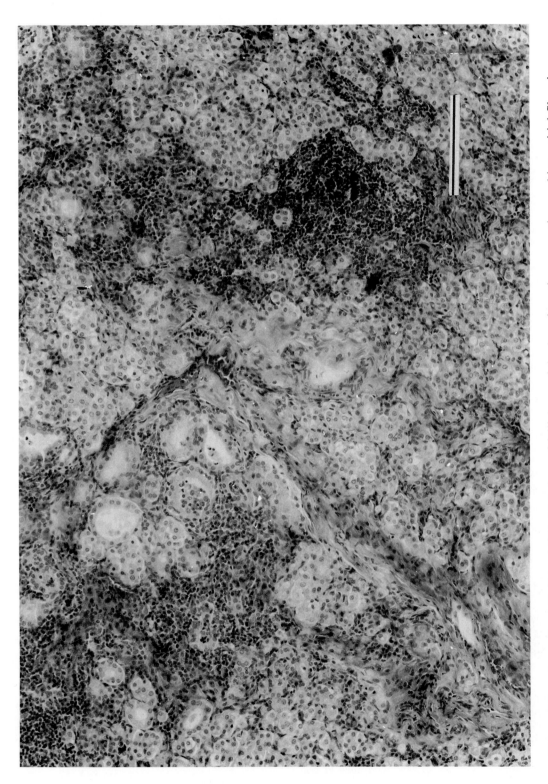

Figure 5.3. Lymphocytic thyroiditis. Note loss of follicles, nodular lymphocytic aggregation, and interstitial fibrosis. *Bar = 200 μm.*

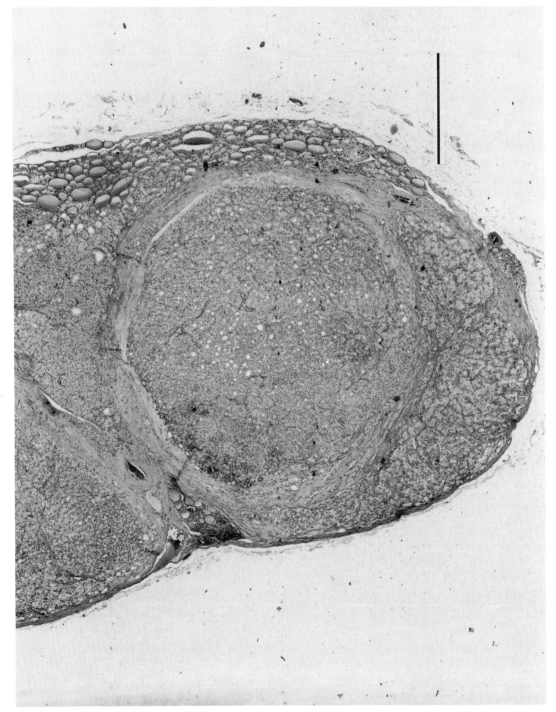

Figure 5.4. Follicular adenoma. Note discrete capsule and compression of surrounding tissue. *Bar = 1000 μm.*

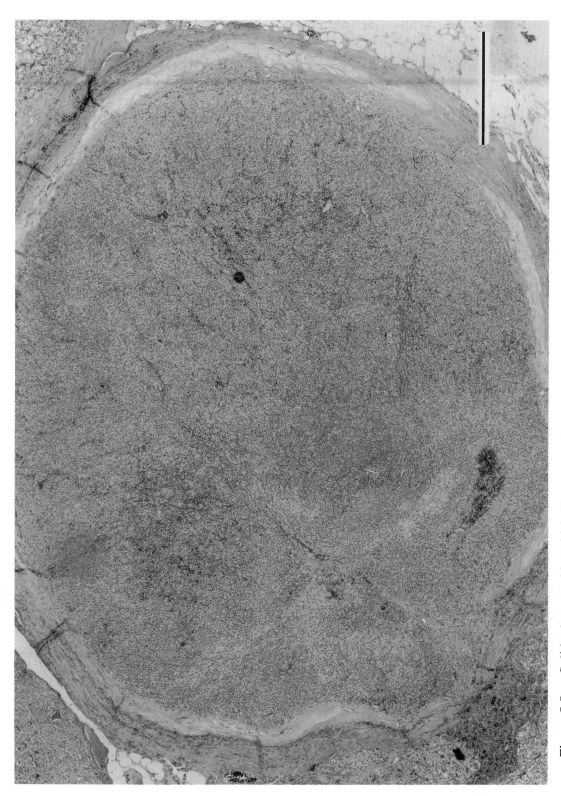

Figure 5.5. Solid adenoma. Note thick fibrous capsule. *Bar = 1000 μm.*

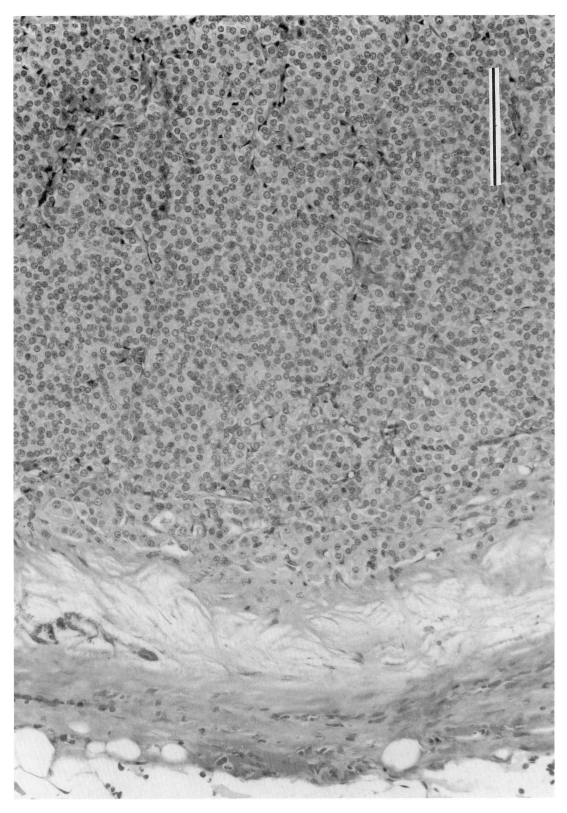

Figure 5.6. **Solid adenoma.** Same lesion as in Figure 5.5, but at greater magnification. *Bar = 200 μm.*

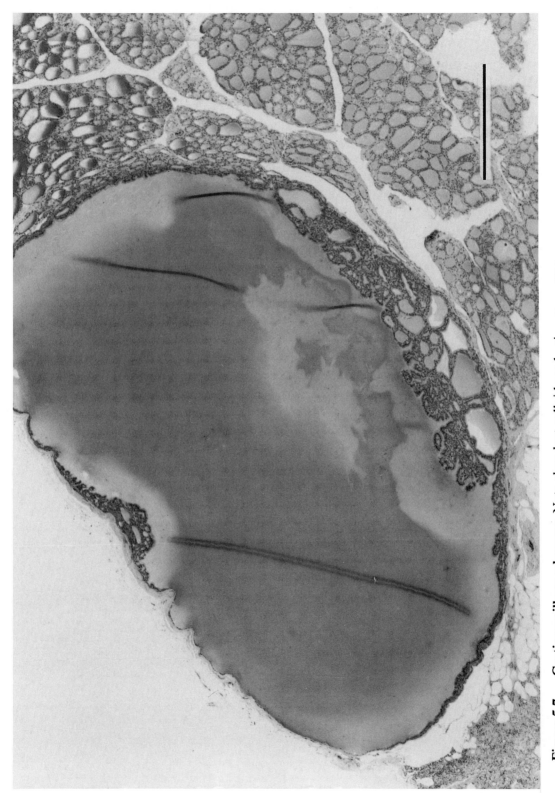

Figure 5.7. Cystic papillary adenoma. Note abundant colloid production. *Bar = 1000 μm.*

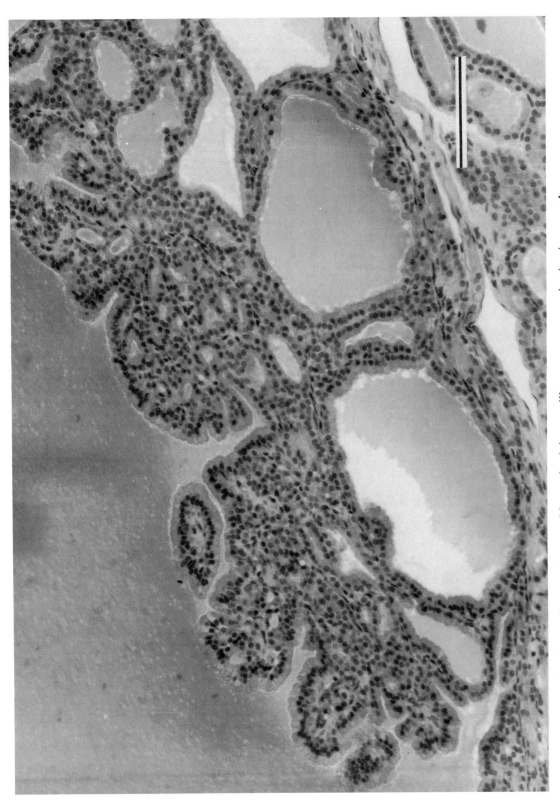

Figure 5.8. Cystic papillary adenoma. Note arborizing papillary structures projecting into cyst lumen. *Bar = 200 µm.*

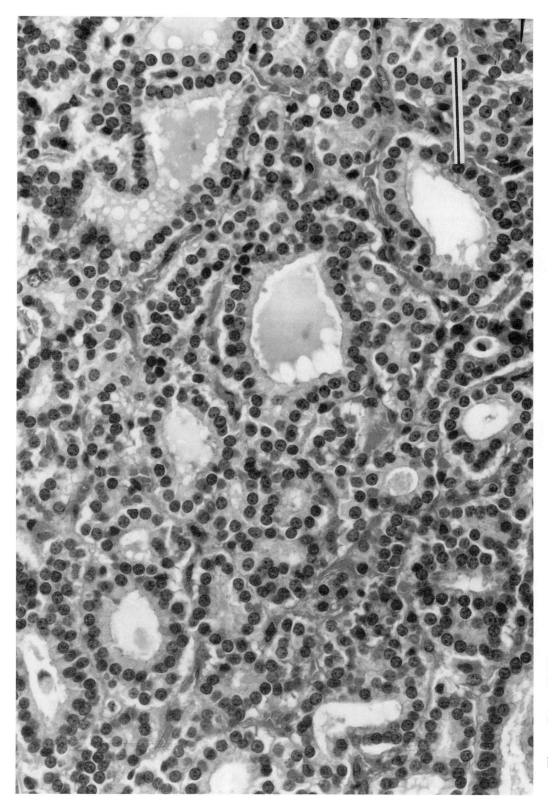

Figure 5.9. Follicular carcinoma. Note predominance of variably sized follicles, only a few of which contain colloid. *Bar = 50 µm.*

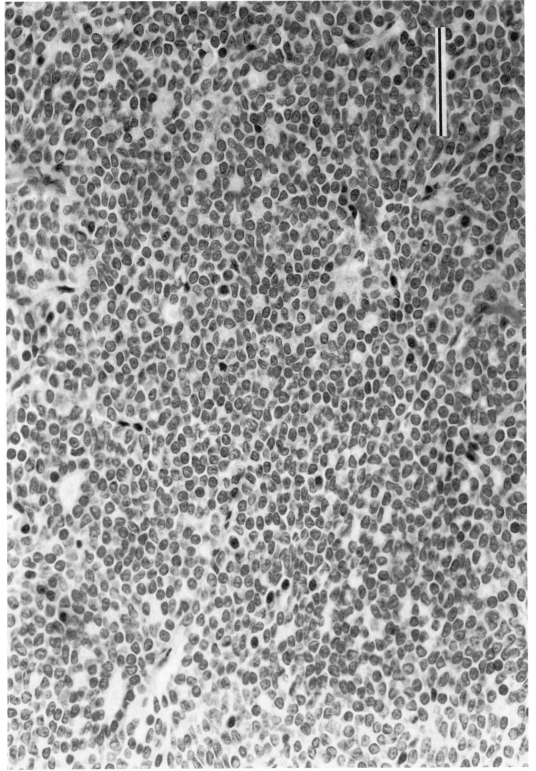

Figure 5.10. **Solid carcinoma.** Note densely cellular sheet of neoplastic cells without follicles or separation into nodular aggregates. *Bar = 50 μm.*

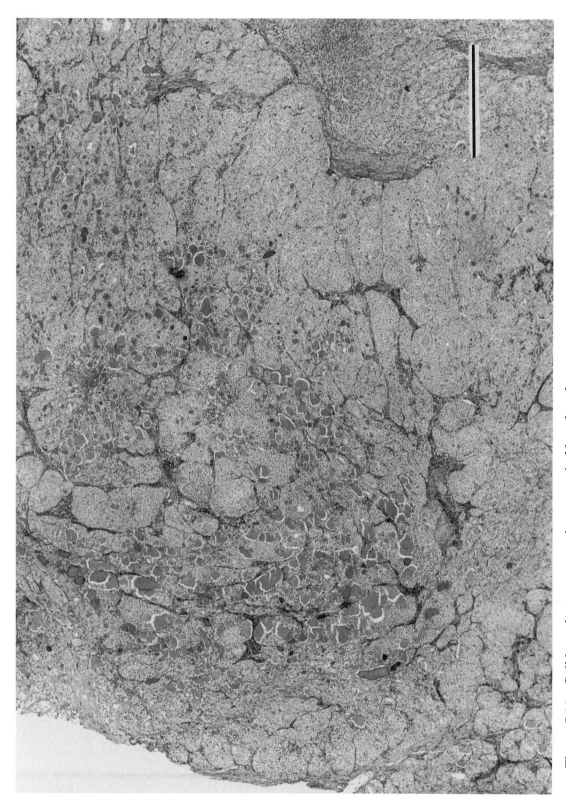

Figure 5.11. Solid carcinoma metastatic to a cervical lymph node. *Bar = 1000 μm.*

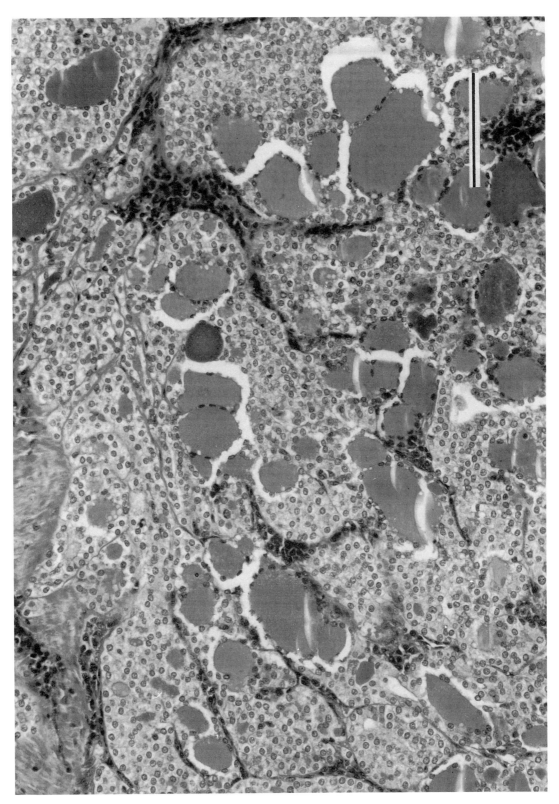

Figure 5.12. **Solid carcinoma with a neoplastic embolus in adjacent vein.** *Bar = 50 μm.*

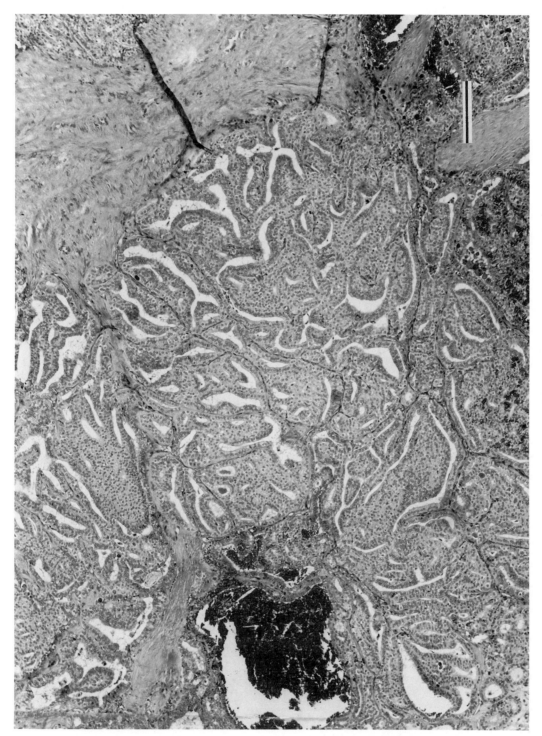

Figure 5.13. Solid follicular carcinoma. Note the presence of both solid and follicular areas. Lymphocytic infiltrates are scattered throughout the mass. *Bar = 1000 μm.*

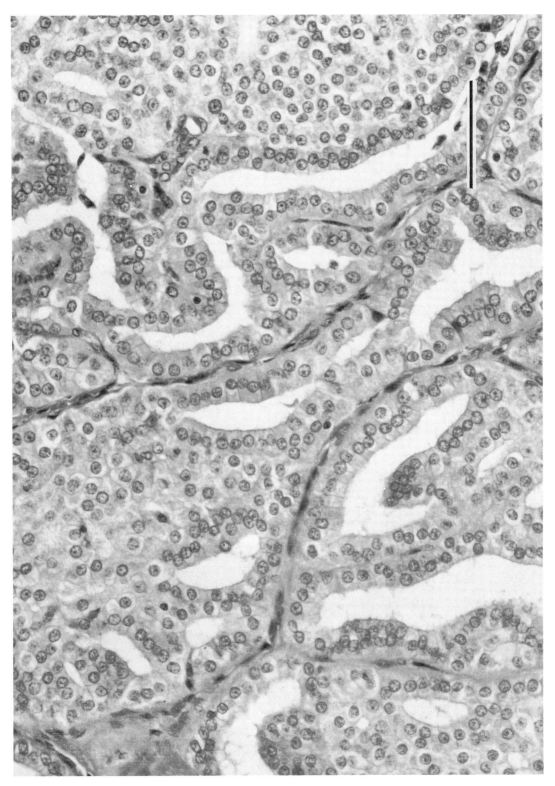

Figure 5.14. **Solid follicular carcinoma.** Same tumor as in Figure 5.13 but at high magnification. *Bar = 200 μm.*

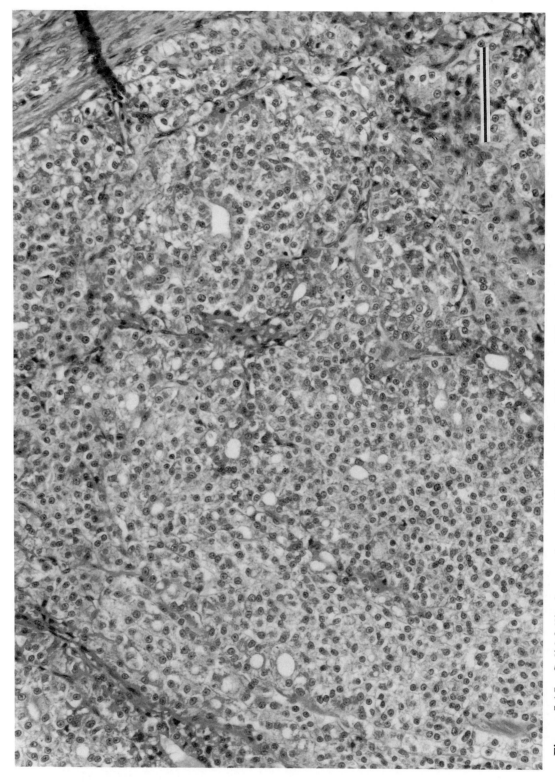

Figure 5.15. Solid follicular carcinoma with an area of papilliferous differentiation. *Bar = 250 μm.*

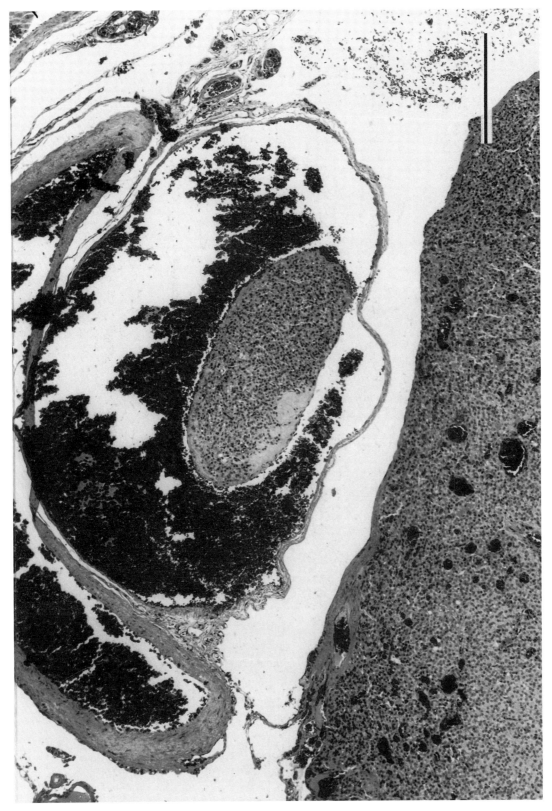

Figure 5.16. **Solid follicular carcinoma.** Same tumor as in Figure 5.15 at higher magnification. *Bar = 200 μm.*

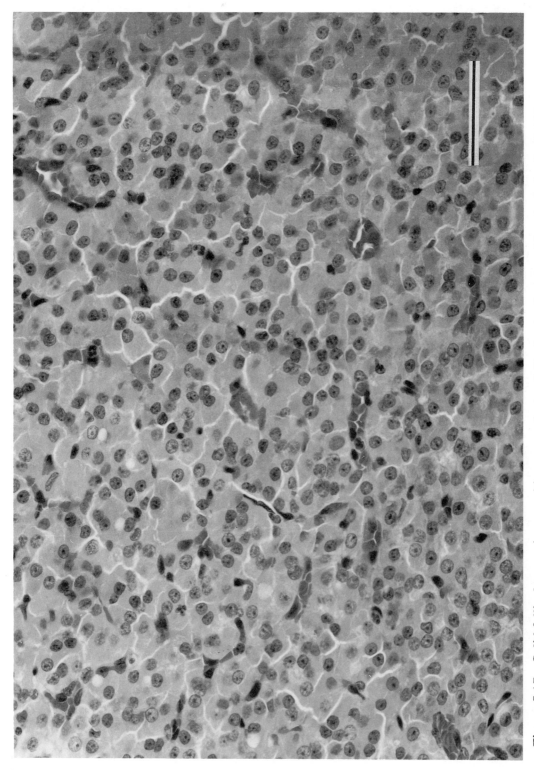

Figure 5.17. Solid follicular carcinoma with an area of microfollicular development. Note the lack of colloid in microfollicles and acinar structures. *Bar = 200 μm.*

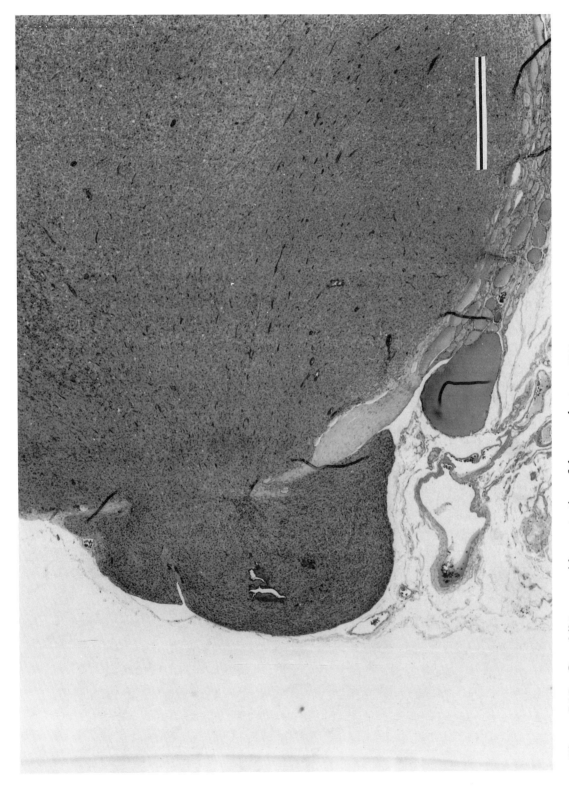

Figure 5.18. Oxyphil tumor with penetration of the capsule. *Bar = 1000 μm.*

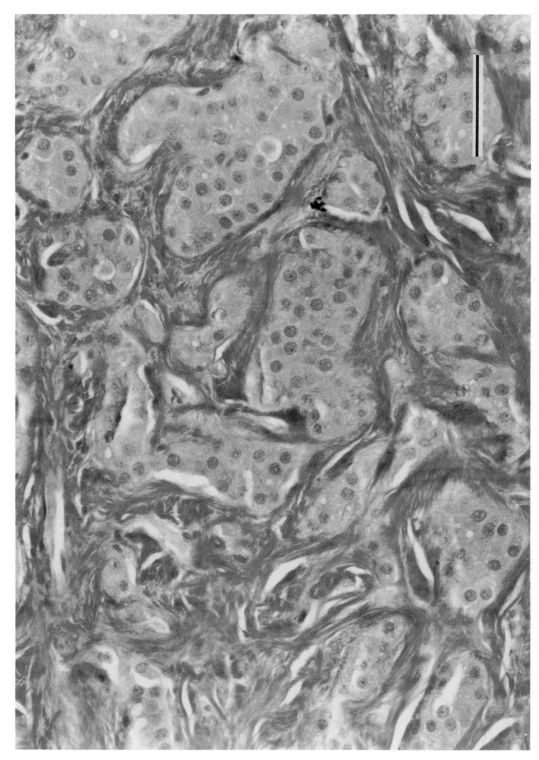

Figure 5.19. **Oxyphil tumor.** Note large polygonal cells with eccentric nuclei and abundant eosinophilic cytoplasm. *Bar = 100 µm.*

APPENDIX

SNOMED Coded Database

Charles R. Watson
National Radiobiology Archives
Pacific Northwest National Laboratory

The authors of this Atlas, in cooperation with the National Radiobiology Archives, are recording their observations in coded form. The glossary of codes is called SNODOG (Watson 1993a,b); it is a beagle-specific extension of the SNOVET (1984) glossary. SNOVET was derived from the Systematized Nomenclature of Medicine (SNOMED 1979, 1982, 1993), which was derived from the Systematized Nomenclature of Pathology (SNOP 1965).

SNOMED is a systematized multiaxial nomenclature of medically useful terms, hierarch-ically organized, where possible, and derived from the basic categories of SNOP. The axes are: Topography, Morphology, Etiology, Function, Disease, Procedure, and Occupation; they are identified by the prefix letter T, M, E, F, D, P, or O in the code. Within an axis, five-character numeric codes are assigned in a hierarchical manner.

SNOVET is a microglossary, or subset, of SNOMED terms applicable to veterinary medicine. The authors of SNOVET added many animal-specific terms, inserting them into the SNOMED numeric hierarchy in the gaps left purposefully for such use. For example, humans do not have tails nor get distemper.

These glossaries were adopted by the DOE laboratories performing long-term studies of beagle dogs at various stages of glossary completion and at various points in time. Each laboratory independently developed computational procedures for handling the codes, and each expanded the glossary to fit research-specific circumstances. For example, neither SNOMED nor SNOVET provided codes for more than two mammary glands, and since mammary tumors are rather common in the beagle, and since beagles have eight mammary glands, each laboratory developed a unique coding system to identify them.

In the late 1980s, the SNODOG glossary was developed to integrate these diverse approaches. The Laboratory for Energy-Related Health Research, University of California at Davis, had made extensive use of SNOMED codes and had added and used a sixth digit in the numeric portion of the codes. Therefore, SNODOG is based on a six-digit code. A master data tape was made, containing every term in the SNOMED and SNOVET glossaries (with a zero appended) and the beagle-specific terms with a 1, 2, 3, ... appended. This tape was distributed to the laboratories and is the standard for information exchange between them and the National Radiobiology Archives. The SNODOG glossary is maintained and coordinated by the Archives; it is revised and distributed periodically as new terms are added (Watson 1993a). Table A.1 illustrates the various codes.

Table A.1 Comparison of Selected Terms in Medical Glossaries

Term	SNOP	SNOMED	SNOVET	SNODOG[a]
Rib (NOS)	T1133	T10350	T10350	T103500
First rib	n/a	T10351	T10351	T103510
Thirteenth rib	n/a	n/a	n/a	T103631
Adrenal gland (NOS)	T9300	T93000	T93000	T930000
Adrenal capsule	T9303	T93030	T93030	T930300
Extracapsular area of adrenal	n/a	n/a	n/a	T930311
X-zone of adrenal gland	n/a	n/a	T93165	T931650
Inflammation	M4000	M40000	M40000	M400000
Inflammation, granulomatous	M4400	M44000	M44000	M440000
Lick granuloma	n/a	n/a	n/a	M440001

[a] Whenever possible SNODOG codes are identical to SNOMED with the addition of shaded 6th character. If no appropriate SNOMED code exists, codes will be introduced in the 5th or 4th character of the most logical SNOMED code.

Pathologists' observations are usually coded as a combination of Topography and Morphology, with occasional use of the other axes. Often, there will be multiple database entries for a given topography code, as it may take several medical terms to describe a particular lesion. Each of the lifespan beagle project laboratories adopted distinct methods of coding observations as described by Watson (1993a). Table A.2 illustrates typical SNODOG coded patholgy observations.

Table A.2 SNODOG-Coded Pathologists' Observations

Description	Topography Code	Morphology Code
Lung Tumor	T280000	M800130
Inflamed prostate gland w/ cystic hyperplasia	T771000	M401020 M730610
Emphysema and fibrosis of the left cardiac lung lobe	T287801	M343010 M480510
Nephrosis	T710000	M531000
Adenocarcinoma, left kidney	T710200	M814030
Radiation pneumonitis	T280000	M116200 M497701

Table A.3 contains the major pathological terms defined in this Atlas, sorted alphabetically. Also shown are the corresponding SNODOG code and standardized nomenclature and the chapter in which the term is discussed. Table A.4 contains the same information as Table A.3, sorted alphabetically by the translation of the SNODOG term. Table A.5 is similar, sorted numerically by SNODOG code. These three tables provide multiple indexes to the atlas and serve as a guide to researchers approaching this information through the databases maintained by the National Radiobiology Archives.

Table A.3 SNODOG Codes and Standardized Nomenclature with Terminology used in the Atlas sorted by Terminology used in Atlas

SNODOG	Standardized Nomenclature	Chapter	Terminology used in Atlas
M81403B	Bronchial adencarcinoma, malignant	4	Adenocarcinoma, Bronchial gland
M814000	Adenoma, benign	4	Adenoma
M81400B	Bronchial adenoma, benign	4	Adenoma, Bronchial gland
M724901	Hyperplasia, adenomatous	4	Adenomatous hyperplasia
M856030	Adenosquamous carcinoma, malignant	4	Adenosquamous carcinoma
M802030	Carcinoma, undifferentiated type, malignant	4,5	Anaplastic carcinoma
M801230	Large cell carcinoma, malignant	4	Anaplastic carcinoma, Large cell
M800230	Tumor, malignant, small cell type	4	Anaplastic carcinoma, Small cell
M844000	Cystadenoma, benign	3	Benign intrahepatic cystadenoma
M825030	Bronchiolo-alveolar adenocarcinoma, malignant	4	Bronchiolavleolar carcinoma
M851030	Medullary carcinoma (C-cell carcinoma), malignant	5	C-cell carcinoma
M824000	Carcinoid tumor, benign	4	Carcinoid tumor, benign
M918130	Chondroblastic osteosarcoma, malignant	1	Chondroblastic Osteosarcoma
M922030	Chondrosarcoma, malignant	1,4	Chondrosarcoma
M918530	Combined osteosarcoma, malignant	1	Combined-Type Osteosarcoma
M807030	Squamous cell carcinoma, malignant (epidermoid carcinoma)	4,5	Epidermoid carcinoma
M984031	Erythremic myelosis	2	Erythremic myelosis (FAB-EM)
M984030	Erythroleukemia, malignant	2	Erythroleukemia (FAB-M6)
M918230	Fibroblastic osteosarcoma, malignant	1	Fibroblastic Osteosarcoma
M881000	Fibroma, benign	4	Fibroma
M881030	Fibrosarcoma, malignant	1,3,4	Fibrosarcoma
M833000	Follicular adenoma, benign	5	Follicular adenoma
M833030	Follicular adenocarcinoma, malignant	5	Follicular carcinoma
M72000F	Hyperplasia, follicular	5	Follicular hyperplasia
M925030	Giant cell tumor of bone, malignant	1	Giant Cell Tumor of Bone
M918630	Giant cell osteosarcoma, malignant	1	Giant Cell Type Osteosarcoma
M912030	Hemangiosarcoma (Angiosarcoma), malignant	1,3,4	Hemangiosarcoma
M817030	Hepatocellular carcinoma, malignant	3	Hepatic cell carcinoma
M580005	Atrophy, follicular	5	Ideopathic follicular atrophy
M816000	Bile duct adenoma, benign	3	Intrahepatic bile duct adenoma
M824030	Carcinoid tumor, malignant	3,4	Intrahepatic carcinoid
M816030	Cholangiocarcinoma (Bile duct carcinoma), malignant	3	Intrahepatic cholangiocarcinoma
M889030	Leiomyosarcoma, malignant	4	Leiomyosarcoma
M885030	Liposarcoma, malignant	1	Liposarcoma
M430000	Inflammation, chronic	5	Lymphocytic thyroiditis

Table A.3 SNODOG Codes and Standardized Nomenclature with Terminology used in the Atlas sorted by Terminology used in Atlas

SNODOG	Standardized Nomenclature	Chapter	Terminology used in Atlas
M961030	Lymphosarcoma, malignant	1	**Lymphosarcoma**
M974030	Mast cell sarcoma, malignant	3	**Mast cell sarcoma**
M991032	Megakaryocytic leukemia with maturation, malignant	2	**Megakaryocytic leukemia with maturation (FAB-M7b)**
M991031	Megakaryocytic leukemia without maturation, malignant	2	**Megakaryocytic leukemia without maturation (FAB-M7a)**
M905030	Mesothelioma, malignant	3,4	**Mesothelioma**
M905000	Mesothelioma, benign	4	**Mesothelioma, benign**
M894000	Mixed tumor (Pleomorphic adenoma), benign	4	**Mixed tumor, benign**
M894030	Mixed tumor, malignant (AFIP 80850)	4	**Mixed tumor, malignant**
M918732	Osteoblastic osteosarcoma, moderately productive, malignant	1	**Moderately Productive Osteoblastic Osteosarcoma**
M989032	Monocytic leukemia with maturation, malignant	2	**Monocytic leukemoa with maturation (FAB-M5b)**
M989031	Monocytic leukemia without maturation, malignant	2	**Monocytic leukemoa without maturation (FAB-M5a)**
M490005	Myelofibrosis	2	**Myelofibrosis**
M986132	Myeloid leukemia with maturation, malignant	2	**Myeloid leukemia with maturation (FAB-M2)**
M986131	Myeloid leukemia without maturation, malignant	2	**Myeloid leukemia without maturation (FAB-M1)**
M986031	Myelomonocytic leukemia, malignant	2	**Myelomonocytic leukemia (FAB-M4)**
M884000	Myxoma, benign	3	**Myxoma**
M884030	Myxosarcoma, malignant	3	**Myxosarcoma**
M720300	Hyperplasia, nodular	3	**Nodular hyperplasia**
M918731	Osteoblastic osteosarcoma, non-productive, malignant	1	**Nonproductive Osteoblastic Osteosarcoma**
M918730	Osteoblastic osteosarcoma, malignant	1	**Osteoblastic Osteosarcoma**
M918030	Osteosarcoma, malignant	1,4	**Osteosarcoma**
M829030	Oxyphilic adenocarcinoma, malignant, primary site	5	**Oxyphil tumor**
M826030	Papillary adenocarcinoma, malignant	4	**Papillary adenocarcinoma**
M826000	Papillary adenoma, benign	4	**Papillary adenoma**
M805030	Papillary carcinoma, malignant	5	**Papillary carcinoma**
M973030	Plasma cell myeloma, malignant	1	**Plasma Cell Myeloma (Multiple Myeloma)**
M918032	Osteosarcoma, poorly differentiated, malignant,	1	**Poorly Differentiated Osteosarcoma**
M918733	Osteoblastic osteosarcoma, productive, malignant	1	**Productive Osteoblastic Osteosarcoma**
M560002	Osteodystrophy, radiation induced	1	**Radiation Osteodystrophy**
M497701	Inflammation, pneumonitis, radiation induced	4	**Radiation pneumonitis**
M964030	Reticulosarcoma (Histocytic Lymphosarcoma), malignant	1	**Reticulum Cell Sarcoma (Histocytic Lymphoma)**
M823030	Solid carcinoma, malignant	4,5	**Solid carcinoma**
M823033	Solid-follicular carcinoma, malignant	5	**Solid-follicular carcinoma**
M724903	Hyperplasia, squamous	4	**Squamous metaplasia**
M918330	Telangiectatic osteosarcoma, malignant	1	**Telangiectatic Osteosaroma**

158

Table A.4 SNODOG Codes and Standardized Nomenclature with Terminology used in the Atlas sorted by Standardized Nomenclature

SNODOG	Standardized Nomenclature	Chapter	Terminology used in Atlas
M814000	Adenoma, benign	4	Adenoma
M856030	Adenosquamous carcinoma, malignant	4	Adenosquamous carcinoma
M580005	Atrophy, follicular	5	Ideopathic follicular atrophy
M816000	Bile duct adenoma, benign	3	Intrahepatic bile duct adenoma
M81403B	Bronchial adencarcinoma, malignant	4	Adenocarcinoma, Bronchial gland
M81400B	Bronchial adenoma, benign	4	Adenoma, Bronchial gland
M825030	Bronchiolo-alveolar adenocarcinoma, malignant	4	Bronchiolavleolar carcinoma
M824000	Carcinoid tumor, benign	4	Carcinoid tumor, benign
M824030	Carcinoid tumor, malignant	3,4	Intrahepatic carcinoid
M802030	Carcinoma, undifferentiated type, malignant	4,5	Anaplastic carcinoma
M816030	Cholangiocarcinoma (Bile duct carcinoma), malignant	3	Intrahepatic cholangiocarcinoma
M918130	Chondroblastic osteosarcoma, malignant	1	Chondroblastic Osteosarcoma
M922030	Chondrosarcoma, malignant	1,4	Chondrosarcoma
M918530	Combined osteosarcoma, malignant	1	Combined-Type Osteosarcoma
M844000	Cystadenoma, benign	3	Benign intrahepatic cystadenoma
M984031	Erythremic myelosis	2	Erythremic myelosis (FAB-EM)
M984030	Erythroleukemia, malignant	2	Erythroleukemia (FAB-M6)
M918230	Fibroblastic osteosarcoma, malignant	1	Fibroblastic Osteosarcoma
M881000	Fibroma, benign	4	Fibroma
M881030	Fibrosarcoma, malignant	1,3,4	Fibrosarcoma
M833030	Follicular adenocarcinoma, malignant	5	Follicular carcinoma
M833000	Follicular adenoma, benign	5	Follicular adenoma
M918630	Giant cell osteosarcoma, malignant	1	Giant Cell Type Osteosarcoma
M925030	Giant cell tumor of bone, malignant	1	Giant Cell Tumor of Bone
M912030	Hemangiosarcoma (Angiosarcoma), malignant	1,3,4	Hemangiosarcoma
M817030	Hepatocellular carcinoma, malignant	3	Hepatic cell carcinoma
M724901	Hyperplasia, adenomatous	4	Adenomatous hyperplasia
M72000F	Hyperplasia, follicular	5	Follicular hyperplasia
M720300	Hyperplasia, nodular	3	Nodular hyperplasia
M724903	Hyperplasia, squamous	4	Squamous metaplasia
M430000	Inflammation, chronic	5	Lymphocytic thyroiditis
M497701	Inflammation, pneumonitis, radiation induced	4	Radiation pneumonitis
M801230	Large cell carcinoma, malignant	4	Anaplastic carcinoma, Large cell
M889030	Leiomyosarcoma, malignant	4	Leiomyosarcoma
M885030	Liposarcoma, malignant	1	Liposarcoma
M961030	Lymphosarcoma, malignant	1	Lymphosarcoma

159

Table A.4 SNODOG Codes and Standardized Nomenclature with Terminology used in the Atlas sorted by Standardized Nomenclature

SNODOG	Standardized Nomenclature	Chapter	Terminology used in Atlas
M961030	Lymphosarcoma, malignant	1	Lymphosarcoma
M974030	Mast cell sarcoma, malignant	3	Mast cell sarcoma
M851030	Medullary carcinoma (C-cell carcinoma), malignant	5	C-cell carcinoma
M991032	Megakaryocytic leukemia with maturation, malignant	2	Megakaryocytic leukemia with maturation (FAB-M7b)
M991031	Megakaryocytic leukemia without maturation, malignant	2	Megakaryocytic leukemia without maturation (FAB-M7a)
M905000	Mesothelioma, benign	4	Mesothelioma, benign
M905030	Mesothelioma, malignant	3,4	Mesothelioma
M894000	Mixed tumor (Pleomorphic adenoma), benign	4	Mixed tumor, benign
M894030	Mixed tumor, malignant (AFIP 80850)	4	Mixed tumor, malignant
M989032	Monocytic leukemia with maturation, malignant	2	Monocytic leukemoa with maturation (FAB-M5b)
M989031	Monocytic leukemia without maturation, malignant	2	Monocytic leukemoa without maturation (FAB-M5a)
M490005	Myelofibrosis	2	Myelofibrosis
M986132	Myeloid leukemia with maturation, malignant	2	Myeloid leukemia with maturation (FAB-M2)
M986131	Myeloid leukemia without maturation, malignant	2	Myeloid leukemia without maturation (FAB-M1)
M986031	Myelomonocytic leukemia, malignant	2	Myelomonocytic leukemia (FAB-M4)
M884000	Myxoma, benign	3	Myxoma
M884030	Myxosarcoma, malignant	3	Myxosarcoma
M918730	Osteoblastic osteosarcoma, malignant	1	Osteoblastic Osteosarcoma
M918732	Osteoblastic osteosarcoma, moderately productive, malignan	1	Moderately Productive Osteoblastic Osteosarcoma
M918731	Osteoblastic osteosarcoma, non-productive, malignant	1	Nonproductive Osteoblastic Osteosarcoma
M918733	Osteoblastic osteosarcoma, productive, malignant	1	Productive Osteoblastic Osteosarcoma
M560002	Osteodystrophy, radiation induced	1	Radiation Osteodystrophy
M918030	Osteosarcoma, malignant	1,4	Osteosarcoma
M918032	Osteosarcoma, poorly differentiated, malignant,	1	Poorly Differentiated Osteosarcoma
M829030	Oxyphilic adenocarcinoma, malignant, primary site	5	Oxyphil tumor
M826030	Papillary adenocarcinoma, malignant	4	Papillary adenocarcinoma
M826000	Papillary adenoma, benign	4	Papillary adenoma
M805030	Papillary carcinoma, malignant	5	Papillary carcinoma
M973030	Plasma cell myeloma, malignant	1	Plasma Cell Myeloma (Multiple Myeloma)
M964030	Reticulosarcoma (Histocytic Lymphosarcoma), malignant	1	Reticulum Cell Sarcoma (Histocytic Lymphoma)
M823030	Solid carcinoma, malignant	4,5	Solid carcinoma
M823033	Solid-follicular carcinoma, malignant	5	Solid-follicular carcinoma
M807030	Squamous cell carcinoma, malignant (epidermoid carcinoma	4,5	Epidermoid carcinoma
M918330	Telangiectatic osteosarcoma, malignant	1	Telangiectatic Osteosaroma
M800230	Tumor, malignant, small cell type	4	Anaplastic carcinoma, Small cell

Table A.5 SNODOG Codes and Standardized Nomenclature with Terminology used in the Atlas sorted by SNODOG Code

SNODOG	Standardized Nomenclature	Chapter	Terminology used in Atlas
M81403B	Bronchial adencarcinoma, malignant	4	Adenocarcinoma, Bronchial gland
M814000	Adenoma, benign	4	Adenoma
M81400B	Bronchial adenoma, benign	4	Adenoma, Bronchial gland
M7224901	Hyperplasia, adenomatous	4	Adenomatous hyperplasia
M856030	Adenosquamous carcinoma, malignant	4	Adenosquamous carcinoma
M802030	Carcinoma, undifferentiated type, malignant	4,5	Anaplastic carcinoma
M801230	Large cell carcinoma, malignant	4	Anaplastic carcinoma, Large cell
M800230	Tumor, malignant, small cell type	4	Anaplastic carcinoma, Small cell
M844030	Cystadenoma, benign	3	Benign intrahepatic cystadenoma
M825030	Bronchiolo-alveolar adenocarcinoma, malignant	4	Bronchiolavleolar carcinoma
M851030	Medullary carcinoma (C-cell carcinoma), malignant	5	C-cell carcinoma
M824000	Carcinoid tumor, benign	4	Carcinoid tumor, benign
M918130	Chondroblastic osteosarcoma, malignant	1	Chondroblastic Osteosarcoma
M922030	Chondrosarcoma, malignant	1,4	Chondrosarcoma
M918530	Combined osteosarcoma, malignant	1	Combined-Type Osteosarcoma
M807030	Squamous cell carcinoma, malignant (epidermoid carcinoma)	4,5	Epidermoid carcinoma
M984031	Erythremic myelosis	2	Erythremic myelosis (FAB-EM)
M984030	Erythroleukemia, malignant	2	Erythroleukemia (FAB-M6)
M918230	Fibroblastic osteosarcoma, malignant	1	Fibroblastic Osteosarcoma
M881000	Fibroma, benign	4	Fibroma
M881030	Fibrosarcoma, malignant	1,3,4	Fibrosarcoma
M833000	Follicular adenoma, benign	5	Follicular adenoma
M833030	Follicular adenocarcinoma, malignant	5	Follicular carcinoma
M72000F	Hyperplasia, follicular	5	Follicular hyperplasia
M925030	Giant cell tumor of bone, malignant	1	Giant Cell Tumor of Bone
M918630	Giant cell osteosarcoma, malignant	1	Giant Cell Type Osteosarcoma
M912030	Hemangiosarcoma (Angiosarcoma), malignant	1,3,4	Hemangiosarcoma
M817030	Hepatocellular carcinoma, malignant	3	Hepatic cell carcinoma
M580005	Atrophy, follicular	5	Ideopathic follicular atrophy
M816000	Bile duct adenoma, benign	3	Intrahepatic bile duct adenoma
M824030	Carcinoid tumor, malignant	3,4	Intrahepatic carcinoid
M816030	Cholangiocarcinoma (Bile duct carcinoma), malignant	3	Intrahepatic cholangiocarcinoma
M889030	Leiomyosarcoma, malignant	4	Leiomyosarcoma
M885030	Liposarcoma, malignant	1	Liposarcoma
M430000	Inflammation, chronic	5	Lymphocytic thyroiditis

Table A.5 SNODOG Codes and Standardized Nomenclature with Terminology used in the Atlas sorted by SNODOG Code

SNODOG	Standardized Nomenclature	Chapter	Terminology used in Atlas
M961030	Lymphosarcoma, malignant	1	Lymphosarcoma
M974030	Mast cell sarcoma, malignant	3	Mast cell sarcoma
M991032	Megakaryocytic leukemia with maturation, malignant	2	Megakaryocytic leukemia with maturation (FAB-M7b)
M991031	Megakaryocytic leukemia without maturation, malignant	2	Megakaryocytic leukemia without maturation (FAB-M7a)
M905030	Mesothelioma, malignant	3,4	Mesothelioma
M905000	Mesothelioma, benign	4	Mesothelioma, benign
M894000	Mixed tumor (Pleomorphic adenoma), benign	4	Mixed tumor, benign
M894030	Mixed tumor, malignant (AFIP 80850)	4	Mixed tumor, malignant
M918732	Osteoblastic osteosarcoma, moderately productive, malignant	1	Moderately Productive Osteoblastic Osteosarcoma
M989032	Monocytic leukemia with maturation, malignant	2	Monocytic leukemoa with maturation (FAB-M5b)
M989031	Monocytic leukemia without maturation, malignant	2	Monocytic leukemoa without maturation (FAB-M5a)
M490005	Myelofibrosis	2	Myelofibrosis
M986132	Myeloid leukemia with maturation, malignant	2	Myeloid leukemia with maturation (FAB-M2)
M986131	Myeloid leukemia without maturation, malignant	2	Myeloid leukemia without maturation (FAB-M1)
M986031	Myelomonocytic leukemia, malignant	2	Myelomonocytic leukemia (FAB-M4)
M884000	Myxoma, benign	3	Myxoma
M884030	Myxosarcoma, malignant	3	Myxosarcoma
M720300	Hyperplasia, nodular	3	Nodular hyperplasia
M918731	Osteoblastic osteosarcoma, non-productive, malignant	1	Nonproductive Osteoblastic Osteosarcoma
M918730	Osteoblastic osteosarcoma, malignant	1	Osteoblastic Osteosarcoma
M918030	Osteosarcoma, malignant	1,4	Osteosarcoma
M829030	Oxyphilic adenocarcinoma, malignant, primary site	5	Oxyphil tumor
M826030	Papillary adenocarcinoma, malignant	4	Papillary adenocarcinoma
M826000	Papillary adenoma, benign	4	Papillary adenoma
M805030	Papillary carcinoma, malignant	5	Papillary carcinoma
M973030	Plasma cell myeloma, malignant	1	Plasma Cell Myeloma (Multiple Myeloma)
M918032	Osteosarcoma, poorly differentiated, malignant,	1	Poorly Differentiated Osteosarcoma
M918733	Osteoblastic osteosarcoma, productive, malignant	1	Productive Osteoblastic Osteosarcoma
M560002	Osteodystrophy, radiation induced	1	Radiation Osteodystrophy
M497701	Inflammation, pneumonitis, radiation induced	4	Radiation pneumonitis
M964030	Reticulosarcoma (Histiocytic Lymphosarcoma), malignant	1	Reticulum Cell Sarcoma (Histocytic Lymphoma)
M823030	Solid carcinoma, malignant	4,5	Solid carcinoma
M823033	Solid-follicular carcinoma, malignant	5	Solid-follicular carcinoma
M724903	Hyperplasia, squamous	4	Squamous metaplasia
M918330	Telangiectatic osteosarcoma, malignant	1	Telangiectatic Osteosaroma

REFERENCES

SNOMED. 1979. Systematized Nomenclature of Medicine, Coding Manual, GE Gantner, RA Cotte, and RS Beckett, Eds. College of American Pathologists, Skokie, IL.

SNOMED. Systematized Nomenclature of Medicine, 2nd edition, updated through 1982. 1982. Volume 1, Numeric Index; Volume 2, Alphabetic Index. College of American Pathologists, Skokie, IL.

SNOMED International. Systematized Nomenclature of Human and Veterinary Medicine, 3rd edition. 1993. Volume 1 and 2, Numeric Index; Volume 3 and 4, Alphabetic Index. RA Côté, DJ Rothwell, JL Palotay, RS Beckett, and L Brochu, Eds. College of American Pathologists, Northfield, IL.

SNOP. Systematized Nomenclature of Pathology. 1965. College of American Pathologists, Skokie, IL.

SNOVET. Systematized Nomenclature of Veterinary Medicine. 1984. Microglossary for Veterinary Medicine, James L Palotay and David J Rothwell, Eds. American Veterinary Medical Association, Schaumburg, IL.

Watson, C.R. 1993a. *SNODOG Glossary, Part I: Introduction*.PNL-8650 Pt. 1, Pacific Northwest Laboratory, Richland, WA.

Watson, C.R. 1993b. *SNODOG Glossary, Part II: Usage of Terms*, PNL-7934, Pacific Northwest Laboratory, Richland, WA, 459 pp.

ACRONYMS

ACHE acetylcholinesterase
ANL   Argonne National Laboratory
CSU   Colorado State University
DOE   U.S. Department of Energy
FAB   French-American-British (system for the classification of acute myeloid leukemia in man)
H&E   Harris hematoxylin and eosin
HH   Harris hematoxylin
ITRI   Inhalation Toxicology Research Institute
MPO   myeloperoxidase
NRA   National Radiobiology Archives
NSE   nonspecific esterose (alpha naphthyl acetate)
OHER Office of Health and Environmental Research
PAS   periodic acid-Schiff
PNNL Pacific Northwest National Laboratory
SNODOG Beagle specific variant of SNOMED created by NRA
SNOMED Systematized Nomenclature of Medicine
SNOP Systematized Nomenclature of Pathology
SNOVET Systematized Nomenclature of Veterinary Medicine
USTUR   U. S. Transuranium and Uranium Registries
W-G   Wright-Giemsa (stain)
WHO World Health Organization
WSU-TC Washington State University—Tri Cities

SUBJECT INDEX

AUTHOR INDEX